EAST LANCASI

EAST LANCASHIRE RAILWAYS

Survival of the Fittest

NIGEL JEPSON

YOUCAXTON
PUBLICATIONS

ISBN 978-1-915972-64-4
Published by YouCaxton Publications 2024

YouCaxton Publications
www.youcaxton.co.uk

Front cover photograph of the Flying Scotsman - courtesy of Tom Moreton
Back cover photograph ELR Long Service Awards Evening October 2021 - courtesy of Mike Kelly's Chairman's Blog

This book is dedicated to Chris Aspin, celebrated author of many works relating to the history of East Lancashire, who sadly passed away in February 2024.

Chris Aspin

'How swift your triumph and how great the power
Of trains that 'flew' at 30 miles an hour'

(Quoted from Chris Aspin's tribute poem of 1966 –
'In *Memoriam: the Stubbins-Accrington Line*')

Acknowledgements

MY THANKS TO ERL/ELRPS officers and staff volunteers alike who have greatly assisted both in terms of providing information and sharing experiences of working on the railway, (in alphabetical order): Pete and Sheila Beetham, Andy Coward, Peter Duncan, David Flood, Andy Hardman, Linda Henderson, John Hopton, Bob Howorth, Mike Kelly, Lee Kenny, Richard and Chandra Law, Glen Newport, Tracey Parkinson, Keith Whitmore, Dave and Margaret Wilson, David Wright.

Similar thanks to those who have helped in a variety of other ways as far as researching the topic, in more general terms, was concerned: Chris Aspin, John Brandrick, Wendy Gradwell (Bury Library), Judith Hilton, John Simpson.

Chris Aspin's inputs have proved particularly valuable, not only on account of his own considerable written output in relation to all things 'East Lancashire' but also his advice relating to this particular study. Lunch meetings with him on Tuesdays at *Park Farm*, Ramsbottom, always proved stimulating to the creative process. Unfortunately, Chris passed away in February 2024, aged 91. This book is dedicated to him.

My thanks also extend to various members of the *Ramsbottom Heritage Society*, in particular bearing in mind his own interest in railways, as so much else, Andrew Todd.

Valuable information towards the writing of the book was gained courtesy of the *National Railway Museum* in York and the *Science Museum* in London. Acknowledgements also on a local level to *Bury, Ramsbottom and Rawtenstall Libraries*.

In addition, appreciation to Bob Fowke and Ella Knight at 'YouCaxton Press' for their helpful and highly constructive input into the production of this book.

Last but certainly not least, enormous gratitude to my wife Anna for her assistance and support - especially technological.

Contents

Sources

Maps & Diagrams

At start of Chapter 2: map showing mid-19th century East Lancashire railway network from 'Accrington and Bacup to Clifton Junction' (acknowledgement to Andrew Young)
Chapter 3: 1) East Lancashire Railway – Bury to Rawtenstall Gradient Profile
Ramsbottom to Accrington line (courtesy of Martin Bairstow)
Ramsbottom to Bacup – Gradient Profile
At start of Chapter 4: East Lancashire Railway - 1859
Chapter 5: Bury to Holcombe Brook – Gradient Profile
At start of Chapter 10: The East Lancashire Railway in modern times
Heywood to Rawtenstall – Gradient Profile
At end of Chapter 12: ELR Gradient Profile – (adapted by AJ Slater from existing diagrams)

Photo Acknowledgements:

First series – p.41: Richard Trevithick's *Catch Me Who Can* – From a contemporary illustration (1808); *Rocket* diagram – From a contemporary drawing in *Mechanics Magazine* (1829); *The Rocket* steam engine, *The Rocket* carriages, statue of George Stephenson – all taken by Anna White at the *National Railway Museum*, York; John Shae Perring – Wikimedia Commons, created 1842: Bury Bolton Street station - *NRM*; Ramsbottom station – *Ramsbottom Heritage Society* collection; '*Choppy*' Warburton and team – Wikimedia Commons, created 1894; '*La Chaine Simpson*' – cartoon by Henri Toulouse Lautrec (1896); Greenmount station – BC Lane collection; Excursion train at Haslingden station – John Alsop collection; Goods Yard Personnel at Bacup station – Bacup Natural History Society; Statue of Sir Nigel Gresley at King's Cross Station, London – Anna White.

Second series - p.89: Beeching – *The Mirror*; Scenes at Clough Fold station, Helmshore station and Police at Summerseat station 1967 – '*Disused Stations*' website; Alan Pegler driving the *Flying Scotsman* with daughter Penny alongside – courtesy of Penny Vaudoyer; 'Last Passenger Train 1972' – Chris Totty; Breaking through barriers – Peter Duncan; Trevor Jones – courtesy of Mike Kelly's *Chairman's Blog*; New Ramsbottom station – Anna White; Rawtenstall station 1992, Irwell Station, *Gothenburg* – courtesy of Mike Kelly's *Chairman's Blog.*

Third series - p.144: *City of Truro* at Heywood station – Raymond Knapman; Scene from filming of '*Coronation Street*' – Andy Coward; Lois Veves unveils award; Burrs Park Plaque, Linda Henderson – first ever female main line locomotive driver); Poster for Wells, Pete Waterman, Long Service Awards evening, Black Horse advert,

Union of South Africa – courtesy of Mike Kelly's *Chairman's Blog*; Father Christmas (aka Pete Beetham) and elf (aka wife Sheila) on *Santa Special* – Pete Beetham; *City of Wells*, Crossing Brooksbottom, *Flying Scotsman* – Tom Moreton; Michael Portillo flanked by ELR members, including Mike Kelly and Richard Law; *Sir Nigel Gresley* – courtesy of Mike Kelly's *Chairman's Blog*.

Introduction

AS A FIRST step in writing about the history of local railways, the book '*The Railway Town of Ramsbottom*' was published last year. However, my aim had always been to write a second book on the theme of railways across East Lancashire as a whole. In this respect, it was encouraging that many people who read the first book said they were looking forward to the 'follow up'. Here it is!

With the intention of painting a picture of railway development across a much broader canvas, the phrase "survival of the fittest" kept springing into mind in relation to how, following the "*railway mania*" of the 1840s, certain railway companies prospered and others went under when the mania calmed down in the 1850s.

Moving forward to the 20th century, in the aftermath of the *Beeching Cuts* of the early 60s, it again seemed interesting to try and pin down why some East Lancashire railway lines survived over time but others did not? For example, what were the significant factors that drove certain groups of rail enthusiasts to mount rearguard actions that enabled them to survive or re-constitute themselves in other forms? Taking the ELR heritage line as a modern-day survivor, what are its chances for the future, bearing in mind present challenges to its existence which are explored in later chapters.

To begin to answer such a series of questions, I felt the need to go back to the "origin of the species" of the early-19th century creation of the railway and evaluate the dynamic effect that, for example, the opening of the Liverpool-Manchester line in 1830 had for the future. Undoubtedly, the miracles achieved by George Stephenson and his *Rocket* had incredible impact at the time, particularly on those who sought to transmute its commercial success to their own spheres of operation elsewhere.

It is hard to appreciate the vast amount of railway-building activity that took place during the 1840s. Up to 1835, there had been only 338 miles of line in existence across the whole country. By 1845, the figure had grown to 2,441 and by 1850 to 6,621 miles. In the single year of 1846, 263 Acts of Parliament were passed for the setting-up of railway lines.

The north-west featured strongly amongst the glut of rail companies coming into existence. For quite some time ahead, there seemed ample scope for all participants in "*railway mania*" to ride the crest of the wave and enjoy profitable outcomes. Predominantly, railway companies experienced strong commercial success during these times with hefty bonuses accruing to shareholders on their financial investments.

For rail passengers, it was an equally positive story. No previous form of transport had ever offered a cheaper, faster or for that matter more exciting form of travel. Similarly, industrialists benefitted handsomely from tapping into such a direct and profitable means of transporting their goods to and from burgeoning factories and mills.

Before long though, the bubble burst.

§

Although the principal focus throughout is on East Lancashire, it became increasingly evident that local developments were affected over time by decisions made at Government level. As decades wore on, neglect of the rail infrastructure set in, allied to central government's preferred strategy of ploughing money into improving roadways for the benefit of car users from the 1930s onwards. In turn, this would lead in the end to ever-more draconian steps being taken to tackle the problems arising out of an accelerating decline in the state of the rail system.

The bitter pill that had to be swallowing during the 1960s came in the form of the so-called '*Beeching Axe*'. Across the country as a whole, 2,363 stations and 5,000 miles of railway line were identified for closure, amounting to 55% of stations and 30% of route miles and the loss of 67,700 British Rail jobs. At the same time, locomotive numbers were to be reduced by 9,000 as well as 16,000 carriages and 450,000 freight wagons. In the face of such a high casualty rate, what were the factors coming into play that caused some stations, some lines and some steam locomotives to survive and others not?

Taking steam locomotives as an endangered species, survival factors seemed largely random, appearing to arise out of chance 'sponsorship' by private enthusiasts, such as Alan Pegler, who stepped forward at the time to save the *Flying Scotsman* from the breaking-yards. Despite the fact that the *Scotsman* still serves today as one of the most miraculous examples of all in terms of longevity on the tracks, virtually all of those who have fought at different times to keep it alive incurred huge financial losses themselves along the way. While the *Scotsman* still runs proudly on East Lancashire lines as an excellent example of "survival of the fittest" in its own right, tribute is paid here to those who incurred incredible financial hardship in the masochistic cause of preserving the majestic *Scotsman.*

Even though the '*Beeching Cuts*' provoked strong local protest action, the Government relentlessly pressed forward in terms of closures of rail lines and stations in East Lancashire, as mirrored across the country as a whole. In such demoralising circumstances, it took guts and great durability on the part of those who held out against the remorseless onslaught. For example, those who formed themselves into the East Lancashire Railway Preservation Society (ELRPS) in the early days must have appreciated the long, uncertain haul they were facing when setting up headquarters at Castlecroft in Bury.

The compelling story is told here of a never-say-die band of volunteers who, despite facing a rocky road along the way, eventually succeeded in opening up a heritage line between Bury and Ramsbottom in 1987.

The present-day East Lancashire Railway heritage line covers a twelve-mile course with its company headquarters based at Bury Bolton Street station, extending from Heywood to Rawtenstall with stations in operation in-between at Bury, Burrs Park, Summerseat, Ramsbottom and Irwell Vale. In commercial terms, the ELR is now a £4m turnover business that succeeds in bringing a similar amount of trade revenue to its local communities. With over 3,600 members at the present time, about 800 of whom actively work as volunteers in a variety of ways, the railway is home to one of the largest fleets of preserved diesel locomotives in the country.

Although the threat posed by Covid appears to have been surmounted, other challenges have arisen in the meantime, such as the spiralling cost of fossil fuels. Affecting all heritage lines equally, speculation remains as to what set of actions might need taking at the present time to safeguard the ELR's future. Above all else, the law of the "survival of the fittest" is a tough one to keep on top of.

Nigel Jepson, July 2024

Chapter One – Stephenson's *'Rocket'* sets the pace

Early Locomotives

At the start of the 19th century, the possibility of making commercial gain from applying steam power to both freight and passenger transport still seemed a remote prospect. Those who pursued the notion were not only unsuccessful but regularly written off as hopeless dreamers. Although William Murdoch had made some progress in the late 18th century, it was his fellow Cornishman Richard Trevithick who gave a first glimpse of what might be achieved in practical terms.

In 1804, Trevithick succeeded in mounting what was credited as the world's first locomotive railway journey when his steam engine hauled a train along the tramway of the Pen-y-Darren iron works, near Merthyr Tydfil in South Wales. By 1808, he had shown further prowess by publicising the merits of a locomotive called '*Catch Me Who Can*' which he ran on a circular track just south of the present-day Euston Square tube station. In entrepreneurial fashion, he sought to capitalise by charging a shilling per passenger ride.

However, for all his pioneering work, Trevithick never passed beyond the experimental stage with railway locomotives, not least because his engines were too heavy for the cast-iron plateway tracks then in use. His fate was to die penniless in 1833, buried in an unmarked grave in St. Edmund's Burial Ground, East Hill, Dartford.

George Stephenson – '*the Father of Railways*'

In 1813, William Hedley built a locomotive which was intended for use on the tramway between Stockton and Darlington. Named *Puffing Billy,* it featured piston rods extending upwards to pivoting beams, connected in turn by rods to a crankshaft beneath the frames which drove the gears attached to the wheels. Showing its durability, *Puffing Billy* remained in service until 1862, when Edward Blackett, the owner of Wylam Colliery, lent it to the *Patent Office Museum* in South Kensington, London (to become the *Science Museum*), later selling it to the museum for £200.

Meanwhile, a year later in 1814, George Stephenson, born in 1781 at Wylam (nine miles to the west of Newcastle-upon-Tyne), made an impressive breakthrough when he designed his first locomotive for hauling coal on the Killingworth colliery wagonway in Northumberland. No doubt *Puffing Billy* exerted an influence on Stephenson's thinking. An early locomotive of his, named *'Blucher'* after the Prussian general who was to fight with the Duke of Wellington at the Battle of Waterloo, succeeded in hauling 30 tons of coal up a hill at 4 mph. *Blucher* was the first effective flanged-wheel adhesion locomotive, its traction depending on contact between its wheels and the rail.

Stephenson, often called *'the Father of Railways'*, proved a shrewd practitioner. Unable to read until he was 18, it did not hold him back in terms of applying natural engineering skills to issues that faced him. At Killingworth, he had worked out by experimentation that half the power of a locomotive was consumed by a line gradient of as little in 1 in 260, concluding that railways should be kept as level as possible. Observance of this principle was to stand him in good stead with regard to his later involvement in the construction of the Liverpool and Manchester Railway (L&MR), involving a series of difficult cuttings, embankments and stone viaducts having to be created in order to level the route.

Stockton-Darlington Line: 1821

In 1821, a bill of parliament was passed which led to the formation of the Stockton and Darlington Railway (S&DR), the first company in the country to operate a combined freight and passenger service. The 25-mile line connected collieries near Bishop Auckland to the River Tees at Stockton, passing through Darlington on the way. While the original intention had been to use horses to draw coal carts on metal rails, company director Edward Pease was persuaded by Stephenson to use locomotive power instead.

Pease and Stephenson jointly established a company in Newcastle to manufacture locomotives. It was set up as *Robert Stephenson and Company*, with George's son Robert the managing director. The rails used for the line, constructed by John Birkinshaw at the *Bedlington Ironworks*, were made out of wrought-iron which could be produced in longer sections and were judged less likely to crack under the weight of heavy locomotives than cast-iron.

The Stockton and Darlington Railway (S&DR) opened officially on 27 September 1825. The engine '*Locomotion No. 1*' hauled an 80-ton load of coal and flour nine miles in two hours, reaching a speed of 24 mph on one stretch. The first purpose-built passenger car, '*Experiment*', was attached which conveyed dignitaries, making it the first time that passenger traffic had been run on a steam locomotive railway line. The gauge of the track was set at 4 feet 8½ inches, later to be adopted as the '*standard gauge*' for railways, not only across Britain but throughout the world.

News of the spectacular nature of the S&DR venture made businessmen sit up and take notice, motivating rich potential investors in the rapidly industrialising North-West to embark upon similar projects of their own.

Bolton-Leigh Line: 1828

Stephenson's services were suddenly in increasing demand beyond his stamping-ground in the north-east. As well as his own expertise being taken up, other trained engineers and workers from the S&DR became involved in the development of lines elsewhere, one of the first being a stretch of nearly eight miles between Bolton and Leigh in Lancashire. For this line, a new locomotive was designed by Robert Stephenson which was far superior to any built previously. The '*Lancashire Witch*' was the first of a new breed of locomotives, achieving unprecedented speeds.

The acclaim with which the new-found power of steam was greeted can be gauged from the report of the *Bolton Chronicle* on the opening of the Bolton and Leigh Railway on 1 August 1828: 'Yesterday having been appointed for the opening of the Bolton to Leigh Railway, a vast concourse of people assembled at an early hour for the purpose of witnessing this interesting and novel spectacle...About a quarter past 12 o'clock the new locomotive constructed by Messrs Stephenson and Co., of Newcastle-upon-Tyne, started from Pendlebury Fold, near Hulton Park. Six waggons were attached to the engine completely filled with gentlemen; also a coach of beautiful structure in which we observed Mr and Mrs Hulton and several other ladies. A number of gentlemen were also upon the roof. There then followed seven other waggons containing ladies and gentlemen and *Bolton Old Band*. The whole weight attached to the engine could not have been less than 40 tons. With this immense weight it proceeded at the rate of seven miles per hour with apparent ease.' [1]

William Hulton (1787-1864) was a landowner, magistrate and coal mine owner. In addition to his family residence at Hulton Park, he owned seven collieries. In 1824, he had become chairman of the Bolton and Leigh Railway Company, which built the first public railway in Lancashire. The line ran to the west of his estate from Bolton to the Leeds and Liverpool Canal in Leigh, enabling him to deliver his coal to market more cheaply. The success of this rail venture acted as a spur to other initiatives being taken in the area, for example the Liverpool and Manchester Railway in 1830.

Liverpool-Manchester Line: 1830

Despite all the progress, there were still many who remained sceptical about what railway locomotives were capable of achieving. Opinion was divided on the respective merits of old-fashioned and new methods of traction. For example, the directors of the Liverpool and Manchester Railway (L&MR) found it difficult to choose between using fixed engines with ropes or steam locomotives on their line. In order to make a better-informed decision, they resolved to hold trials to see if a steam locomotive would best meet their requirements, staging a prize competition from 6 to14 October 1829. These were the so-called '*Rainhill Trials*', in which five locomotives vied to prove most successful in completing a trial course along a 1 mile (1.6 km) length of track.

Stephenson's *'Rocket'* was an early *0-2-2* locomotive which was built very much with the *Rainhill Trials* in mind and demonstrating that improved mobile locomotives were more efficient than stationary steam engines. *'Rocket'* had a tall 16 feet smokestack chimney at the front, a cylindrical boiler in the middle, and a separate firebox at the rear. It won the competition averaging 12 mph (19km/h) and achieving a blistering top speed of 30 miles per hour (48 km/h) hauling 13 tons, and was declared the winner of the £500 prize (over £45,000 in today's values). Following their success, the Stephensons were given the contract for supplying locomotives to the L&MR.

The L&MR was the first modern railway of its kind, in that both the goods and passenger traffic were operated by scheduled or timetabled locomotive-hauled trains. Although the promoters were mainly interested in goods traffic, they were pleasantly surprised to find that passenger traffic might also prove a lucrative source of profit.

The opening of the L&MR line took place on 15 September 1830 with the guest of honour being the Prime Minister, the Duke of Wellington. For the principal guests, the company provided 'a costly and splendid car' 32 feet long and 8 feet wide and carrying a 'lofty canopy of crimson cloth' which rested on eight carved and gilt pillars. Ornamental gilt balustrades, scrolls and ducal coronets added to the splendour. A rich crimson-covered ottoman provided seats for 30 people and 'the whole had a magnificent and imposing effect in the Grecian style of architecture.' [2]

One of the travellers, Fanny Kemble, a noted writer and actress of the time, recounted the occasion in the first volume of her memoirs: 'Enormous masses of densely packed people lined the road, shouting and waving hats as we flew by them. What with the sight and sound of these cheering multitudes and the tremendous velocity with which we were borne past them, my spirits rose to the true champagne height and I never enjoyed anything so much as the first hour of our progress.' [3]

The celebrations didn't last long though. Tragedy struck when, seventeen miles into the journey away from Liverpool, the train procession stopped at Parkside to enable the engines to take on a fresh supply of water. Amongst passengers alighting from the train at this point was William Huskisson, MP for Liverpool and a former President of the Board of Trade. Approaching the Duke's carriage to pay his respects, he failed to note the *Rocket* speeding up the track upon which he stood. Warnings were shouted to Huskisson to stand clear, but he had seemed confused, instead attempting a further step towards the Duke's carriage. The engine hit him full on, crushing a leg. Accompanied by his wife, Huskisson was conveyed to Eccles Vicarage, near Manchester, to be treated by doctors. However, his wounds were so severe that he died just after 9 p.m. that evening.

In the midst of the deep gloom descending straightaway, the Duke of Wellington desired the train to return to Liverpool. However, the chief municipal officer of Manchester, the borough reeve, warned him that the disappointed masses awaiting his arrival in Manchester might react in an ugly way. Reluctantly continuing, the onward journey was to prove no easier. First of all, an angry mob of protesters was lying in wait on the track three miles out of Manchester with the intention of protesting to the Prime Minister against the hated *Corn Laws*, legislation protecting home landowners against competition from cheaper imports of produce from abroad. Widespread hardship was caused by poor people not being able to afford to buy food.

Despite the train somehow forcing its way through, to the Duke's consternation, there was another even larger group of protesters waiting on the Manchester station platform. Those dignitaries who tried to reach the company's warehouses, where a served meal was waiting, found themselves in the firing line of verbal insults as well as having stones and lumps of clay hurled at them. When the chief of the Manchester police received information that yet more protesters were about to advance to the bridge near to where the carriages were standing, the Duke was warned that if he did not leave immediately, the chief would not answer for the consequences. Shortly after, to the great relief of police and company officials alike, the train procession stole out of the station and out of immediate harm's way.

Even though the occasion had ended sourly on the day, there was to be no doubting the longer-term success of the Liverpool and Manchester Railway, especially in economic terms. The merchants and manufacturers, who had promoted the line as a more productive and efficient form of transport than canals, quickly reaped benefits from their enterprise. The company's directors must have enjoyed reading reports in newspapers such as the following one that described the new massive increase in volume of trade: 'On Friday, four journeys were accomplished each way, one of which was performed by a connected train of three engines and twenty-four waggons, which brought to this town between 80 and 90 tons of goods!!' [4]

Lack of Rules and Regulations

With the emphasis given to looking to make profit, very few regulations were put in the way of running railways in those early times. Along the L&MR for example, impromptu stops took place for refreshments. 'At Eccles, villagers waited for trains with Eccles cakes, while public houses beside the line did brisk business by sending out trays of drinks and cigars...Engine-drivers and firemen had to contend with bad weather and smoke – there were no enclosed cabs – and a highly unreliable signalling system. Sharing the engine crews' miseries were the third-class passengers who were herded like cattle – and sometimes with cattle – in open waggons (so-called '*Parliamentary trains*') with standing room only.' [5]

Following the 1840 *Act for Regulating Railways*, which empowered the Board of Trade to appoint railway inspectors, there was growing awareness of the need for the government to adopt certain basic measures to monitor the development of railways. A Railway Inspectorate was established in the same year with powers to enquire into the causes of accidents and recommend ways of avoiding them.

However, company 'rules and regulations' at this time illustrate the rudimentary way in which potential dangers were handled on the ground. For example, in one handbook it is stated: 'If it be required to warn an engineman or guard to stop a train, then the signal made for this purpose in the day time must be, to wave a red flag or a hat UP AND DOWN (up to the height of the head and then to the ground).

Meanwhile Rule XX, drawn up especially for use 'during fog or thick weather', instructed the engine driver, on stopping a passenger train in a station 'to send someone (likely to be his 'guard') to run back 400 yards behind the train, or so far as may be necessary to warn any coming engine, in order to prevent its running against the other.' [6]

The guard in these early days travelled on the roof where he was subjected to cruel treatment from the dictates of the weather, smoke and, if unwary, low tunnels. It was not until the later 1840s that the guard was to be placed inside the train in 2nd or 3rd class carriages.

As basic as these measures sound, they were typical of the pioneering early times of railway operation. Entrepreneurs put far higher priority on profit-making than health and safety.

'Railway Mania'

The period of development which opened up in the 1840s later became known as the decade of '*Railway Mania*'. Coinciding with an economic up-turn, manufacturing industries such as cotton were in a strong position to speed up production. Railway companies boomed, at the same time encouraging waves of new investment.

Although the Liverpool and Manchester is often seen as the first 'modern' railway, it had started out in 1830 as a self-contained 35-mile track designed merely to link the two major towns in question. The first proper trunk line, the Grand Junction Railway, was opened in 1837 linking the Liverpool and Manchester Railway with Birmingham, via Crewe, Stafford and Wolverhampton.

Throughout this early period of time, the Government did not see fit to put any obstacles in the path of new railway ventures. With minimal regulation, any group of individuals could form a company, seek to gain investment and then submit a bill to Parliament in order to gain the right to acquire land for the route of the proposed railway. Since many MPs themselves were heavy investors in such schemes, it was exceedingly rare for Parliament to reject a bill.

Manchester-Bolton Line: 1838

As early as 1830, the Manchester, Bolton and Bury Canal Company had sought to promote the construction of a railway along the line of their canal from Salford to Bolton and onwards to Bury in East Lancashire. An Act of Parliament was passed to enable them to become a railway company with the original plan being to connect up all three centres by rail. However, the line was destined not to go as far as Bury after the company's engineer, Jesse Hartley, decided that the many engineering feats needing to be undertaken, including for example a 1,100 yard tunnel on a gradient of 1 in 100, were too expensive to carry out. In these circumstances, Bury was left out of the equation. The opening of the Manchester-Bolton line took place on 29 May 1838. It was to continue functioning as an independent concern until 18 August 1846 when it was amalgamated with the Manchester and Leeds Railway.

Manchester-Leeds Line (together with branch lines): 1841

By 1841, a 51-mile rail route had been built connecting Manchester and Normanton, where it joined the route of the north Midland Railway (another of George Stephenson's lines which ran from Derby to Leeds) which meant there was now in effect connection between Manchester and Leeds. There were also many branch line connections, for example in East Lancashire, the Heywood branch. Heywood was an important industrial centre at this time with numerous cotton mills and an iron foundry. A 1¾ mile single line branch was constructed to Heywood from where Castleton lay on the main line. At this time, the locality was known as Blue Pits (sometimes spelt 'Pitts'), two miles south-west of Rochdale. It cost £10,000 (about £21 million in modern-day values) to build and opened on 15 April 1841. The branch trains relied at first on horse traction until a locomotive was put to use on the line from 1 May 1847 onwards.

Bury/Rossendale threatened with isolation

From there having been only 338 miles of line in existence across the whole country up to 1835, the rapid expansion of rail transport can be measured by the fact that by 1845 the figure had grown to 2,441 and by 1850 to 6,621 miles. In the single year of 1846, 263 Acts of Parliament were passed for the purpose of setting up new railway lines.

Whereas canals had provided competition to start with, railways quickly gained the upper hand as a preferred and more lucrative means of transport. There was now no greater danger to an industrial district than to remain unconnected to the rail network and suffer the fate of being reduced to a commercial backwater. Unfortunately, this was the prospect now facing the Bury/Rossendale district of East Lancashire.

Notes

1. *Bolton Chronicle*, 1 August 1848
2. *Liverpool Courier*, 16 September 1830
3. Fanny Kemble, *Journal – Volume 1*, 1835 p.135
4. *Manchester Chronicle*, January 1831
5. Chris Aspin, *The First Industrial Society – Lancashire 1750-1850,* pub. Carnegie 1995 pp. 32-33
6. Manchester and Bolton Railway Company 1841, quoted in Chris Aspin, *The First Industrial Society* p.36

Chapter Two – Local industrialists take the initiative

Important meeting at the *Red Lion Inn* in Bury

By 1843, it had become abundantly clear that the Manchester, Bolton & Bury Canal Navigation & Railway Company was not going to continue its railway scheme as far as Bury. In such circumstances, on 14 September 1843, 'the initiative was assumed by a group of "influencial inhabitants" of the town of Bury who met at the *Red Lion Inn* in Bury, a hostelry which used to stand next to the Priory Church'. [1]

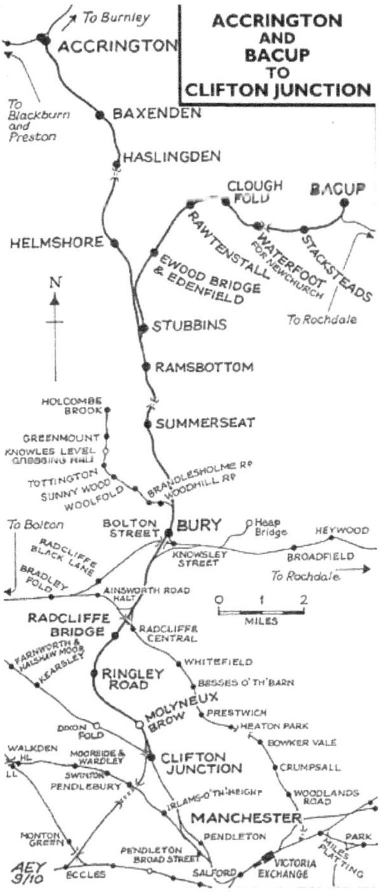

Accrington and Bacup to Clifton Junction

At this meeting, it was agreed that the project of building a railway between Manchester, Bury and Rawtenstall was 'worthy of being entertained'. A provisional committee was set up consisting of Thomas Wrigley, John Grundy, Richard Walker MP, John Robinson Kay, Henry Hoyle Hardman,

David Whitehead, together with members of Ramsbottom's Ashton family. [2]

It is interesting to note how strongly the membership of this committee reflected the geography and nature of industry in and around Bury. For example, Thomas Wrigley was a Bury cotton mill owner and was destined in the mid-1840s to take over family responsibility for the *Bridge Hall Paper Mills* at Heap Bridge, close to Bury. This was to become one of the largest paper mills in the world, stretching for half-a-mile along the banks of the River Roch.

John Grundy was another paper manufacturer from this same district. Thomas Wrigley forged a close working relationship with the Grundy family who ran the nearby *Heap Bridge Mill.* Reflecting the closeness of the two families, there were at least five marriages between the Wrigley's and the Grundy's during these times. The Bury area had developed as a major papermaking centre on the back of mills providing a steady supply of cotton waste. The same industry became a leading customer for paper by using it for packing.

Richard Walker had been the Liberal MP for Bury since 1832 and was the eldest son of William Walker, a woollen manufacturer and original head of the family firm of William Walker & Sons of Stanley Street Bury. John Robinson Kay was the owner of mills at Brooksbottoms in Summerseat and also at Rawtenstall. Henry Hoyle Hardman, son of George Hardman, at this time shared part-ownership with his brother Edward of his father's wool mill in New Hall Hey, Rawtenstall. David Whitehead was a major figure in the cotton industry, developing several mills in Rawtenstall. These three industrialists gave powerful added voice to the argument in favour of extending the line through Rossendale as far as Rawtenstall.

The Ashtons owned *Ramsbottom Mill,* sited on Crow Lane in Ramsbottom. By the 1830s, this mill, under Samuel and Thomas Ashton, had become the biggest in the Irwell Valley with three enormous waterwheels and three powerful steam engines. Although there is no record of any of the Grant Brothers serving on the original committee, they too were prominent mill-owners in Ramsbottom and would no doubt have supported the case for making Ramsbottom an important stopping-off point on the line between Bury and Rawtenstall.

Another major backer was Thomas Aitken, a cotton manufacturer who by this time owned two mills, one in Chatterton, near Stubbins, and the other in Irwell Vale. The former-mentioned site had notoriously been the location of the so-called *Chatterton Riot* of 1826. In that year, an angry mob of workers, despite local Justice of the Peace William Grant having read out the Riot Act, went on to smash newly-installed labour-saving power looms at the mill. This incurred a reaction from the assembled military that had led to the death of six people. Moving forward though to the present, Thomas Aitken was to subscribe £2,500 to the railway scheme and become one of the original directors of the soon-to-be-formed company.[3]

Establishment of the Manchester, Bury and Rossendale Railway

It was agreed at the meeting at the *Red Lion* to set up a company assuming the title of 'The Manchester, Bury and Rossendale Railway'. A follow-up meeting took place shortly afterwards at the *Eagle and Child Inn* in Bury on 29 September. Richard Walker acted as chairman. The results of a traffic count were made known to the gathering. From this survey, it was noted that '6,000 people travelled by some kind of conveyance along Manchester Road per week and it was estimated that the revenue for passengers and goods between Manchester and Rawtenstall would result in a dividend of 10% on the proposed capital of £300,000 (roughly the equivalent of £32 million in modern day terms) to be raised by 12,000 shares, with a value of £25, requiring a deposit of £2.50 per share.' [4]

The initial purpose was to construct a double track railway from Clifton, forming a junction with the Manchester and Bolton line. This then opened up the possibility of extending the line northwards from Bury along the Irwell Valley to reach Rawtenstall via Ramsbottom. At the same time, the committee appreciated that the intentions of other railway companies operating in the area needed to be taken into account, for example the Manchester and Leeds Railway which at this point in time was seeking to extend its Heywood branch to Bury.

Without doubt, local industrialists pulled the strings in terms of railway development in the area. Planning around the operation was geared pivotally around providing enhanced transport connections to and from factories and mills. This same factor dictated elements of infrastructure such as deciding upon the location of stations and sidings en route.

Formation and Development of the East Lancashire Railway Company

Complications arose as to the route the new railroad might take. Two alternative proposals were put forward, one the MB&RR's own and another which had been devised by the Manchester and Leeds Railway (M&LR). The former looked to join the Manchester and Bolton Railway at Clifton, the latter going for a linking with the M&LR line heading out from Collyhurst.

Fortunately, for the MB&RR, the Earl of Derby, who owned much of the land in question, favoured the Clifton Junction route. In due course, a bill was presented to Parliament for a double line from Clifton Junction to Bury and a single line onward to Rawtenstall. Opposing this, the M&LR presented a bill of its own: one aimed at connecting up the line to Bury at Collyhurst, approaching from the direction of Heywood. Both bills received a second reading in the House of Commons in March 1844 but the M&LR bill was rejected at Committee stage. On 4 July 1844, the private bill put forward by the MB&RR was given Royal Assent. The Act authorised the company to raise £300,000 (equivalent of £32 million in modern-day values), and also granted the right to borrow £100,000.

As previously stated, the Government rarely put obstacles in the path of new railway ventures in these early days. Facing minimal regulation, any group of individuals could form a company, seek to gain investment and then submit a bill to Parliament in order to gain the right to acquire land for the route of the proposed railway. Although it was exceedingly rare for Parliament to reject a bill, the trickier part for rail entrepreneurs was to convert the terms of their bill into financial profit on the ground.

Two surveyors, Thomas Gooch and Charles Cawley were appointed to map out the precise route from Clifton Junction through to Rawtenstall. Thomas Gooch, born in 1808, was from Bedlington in Northumberland and had previously been apprenticed to George Stephenson. He had been Stephenson's assistant in the surveying of the route for the Manchester and Leeds railway. Charles Cawley was a local East Lancashire man, born at Middleton in 1812. He had worked before with Gooch, superintending construction at the Manchester end of the M&LR line.

Following the survey, a plan was devised to build the railway line to run north from Clifton through a cutting at Outwood, requiring the removal of about 600,000 cubic yards (460,000 cubic metres) of earth. From this point, the line would pass north-east through Radcliffe Bridge and then into Bury Bolton Street station. From Bury, it was to pass through Summerseat, Ramsbottom, Stubbins, Ewood Bridge and finally on to Rawtenstall. It was appreciated that the railway needed to climb a constant gradient, calling for several engineering feats to be carried out, including a variety of viaducts, tunnels, cuttings and embankments. [5]

Reflecting the frenzied approach to railway-building at the time, simultaneous projects were being discussed in surrounding districts to the north of Bury and Rossendale, regarding the laying of other lines. For example, plans for a 'Blackburn, Burnley, Accrington & Colne Extension Railway' were being hatched. Despite the rivalry and in-fighting that often went on between the various interest groups, a growing awareness developed as to the potential advantages of an amalgamation.

At a meeting on 17 October 1843, a group of landowners, merchants and traders from Accrington had sought to convince the provisional committee of the MB&RR that their undertaking should extend to Accrington via a continuation of the line from Stubbins Junction (situated between Ramsbottom and Rawtenstall) northwards to meet the west-to-east Preston to Burnley route at Accrington.

This proposed further extension was authorised by an Act of Parliament of 30 June 1845. With the two companies seeing eye-to-eye, an amalgamation came about by further Act of Parliament on 24

July 1845, at which point in time the MB&RR absorbed the other company, whilst trading from now on under the heading of the East Lancashire Railway.

Almost immediately afterwards, the ELR negotiated terms to further incorporate the Blackburn and Preston Railway. By October 1845, the empire had also absorbed the embryonic Liverpool-Ormskirk Railway. The scale of ambition involved in taking on such a huge challenge was even more immense for the fact that all these different lines under discussion were hardly beyond the drawing board stage at this point in time

Operational Challenges

Meanwhile, the contract for constructing the Clifton to Rawtenstall section had been awarded in May 1844 to Pauling and Henfrey, Manchester-based contractors. This firm had recently become involved in building new barracks on Bolton Road in Bury which the Government had wanted constructed quickly in order to have soldiers stationed in the area to combat widespread social unrest at this time brought on by the onset of protest groups such as the Chartists. [6]

On 12 August 1844, John Hawkshaw was appointed consulting engineer, a man whose services were much sought after at this time. He did not last long in post though, resigning in December 1844 due to an existing obligation of his to support the M&LR extension from Heywood to Bury. In the same year, the position of assistant engineer had been taken up by John Shae Perring, who was to become ELR's chief engineer from May 1846 onwards.

Pauling and Henfrey's tender had amounted to £167,529 (equivalent to £17m today), that was accepted in the form of two separate contracts, firstly from Clifton to Bury and secondly from Bury to Rawtenstall/Accrington. It was the usual custom for large-scale contractors like Pauling and Henfrey to sub-let to smaller contractors who undertook to carry out different sections of the work. For example, projects were sub-let to John Kellett at Radcliffe and John Heywood at Nuttall Tunnel, close to Ramsbottom. [7]

The hilly nature of the terrain posed major challenges. For example at Clifton, the line had to cross the Irwell valley on a viaduct of thirteen arches, including one of 96-feet (28.8m) span with a height of 80 feet (24m) over the river. Near Radcliffe, the Irwell had to be re-crossed at a height of 70 feet (21m) on a wooden viaduct on stone piers, with five spans of 55 feet (16.5m). A mile short of Bury, the river was crossed for the third time by an iron bridge of 100 feet-span (30m).

Translating plans into action went anything but smoothly. The first problem during the summer of 1845 was a worker recruitment crisis. Given the amount of railway lines that were being built up and down the country at this time, it was perhaps no real surprise that such problems arose. Measures were taken to offset the shortfall but these sometimes proved counter-productive. For example, seven men who had complied with an arrangement to work Sundays had ended up being charged with the offence of breaking the Sabbath. [8]

The winter of 1845/6 saw continuous wet weather which made levelling up land most challenging. Landslips occurred and embankments were washed away as quickly as they had been mounted up. However, by the start of 1846, the recruitment crisis had eased and before long 700 'navvies' (a term borrowed from the 'navigator' work-force that had built the canals) were engaged working on the line between Bury and Rawtenstall.

It was far from plain sailing for employers though with troubles flaring up at times between different sections of the work-force. In May 1846 for example, an episode was reported in the *Manchester Guardian* in which: 'an alarming riot took place among the labourers on the East Lancashire Railway at Ramsbottom. Disturbances arose from a dispute respecting wages between two English and two Irish labourers (in the *Grant Arms*) who, as previously jealousy had existed between the two nations, succeeded in enlisting their respective countrymen into the quarrels and nearly 2,000 men were at one time engaged. Many men on both sides were severely beaten and a number of Irish were driven from their homes...previously to the arrival from Bury of the police under Inspector McDonald who succeeded in dispersing the riot. The police remained on duty all night and yesterday all was perfectly quiet.' [9]

The occasion of monthly pay-outs often led to serious disturbances when, with money in their pockets, the 'navvies' went out on an extended 'randy'. Without question, these men habitually worked hard but when the opportunity came to carouse, they drank and played even harder. In a telling description of their general attitude to life, it was said that 'they were heathens, in the heart of Christian people, savages in the midst of civilisation and it is scarcely an exaggeration to say, that a feeling something akin to that which awed the Roman when the Goth was at his gates, opened up in the minds of those citizens near where the railway labourer pitched his tent... they lived only for the present; they cared not for the past and were indifferent to the future.' [10]

Further difficulties arose when chief contractors Pauling and Henfrey were charged with misleading the Company about how much time was needed to construct the line. With progress slipping behind schedule, Pauling and Henfrey were sacked and the contract given to John Waring. This firm had stronger experience of building railways, for example for the York and North Midland. To add insult to injury for Pauling and Henfrey, much of their equipment was seized off them by way of extracting compensation.

The Process of Land Purchase

On the positive side, the ELR had experienced relatively few problems to date in purchasing the land it required. Tithe surveys of the time confirmed that much of the land along the projected route was made up of 'waste, woodland, pasture or reservoirs, except at Brooksbottoms (described locally as *Brox)* where arable land was avoided by the tunnel'. [11]

The chief landowner along the route was the Earl of Derby. His family was long-established in the area. In the 15th century, the title had been conferred on the present incumbent's ancestor Thomas Stanley by King Henry VII after the Battle of Bosworth in 1485 at which, against all the odds, Henry had defeated the existing king, Richard III. Having given much-needed military support to the claimant to the throne, Thomas' reward had been to inherit swathes of land in the Bury area, formerly owned by the Pilkington family who paid the price for backing Richard. Thomas Pilkington had been captured and killed, after which his lands had been confiscated and presented to the Derby family, in whose hands they had remained ever since.

The present-day Earl of Derby quickly latched on to the fact there were healthy profits to be gained with the ELR needing to buy the land off him, levying a sum of £400 per acre for his land. The going rate for anyone with less exalted status appeared to be about half this amount.

Response of other Landowners

Above all else, the ELR had been mindful 'not to wish to inflame the good will of the mill owners'. For their own part, influential 'manufacturers' such as John Robinson Kay sought not only to protect the land his business premises stood on but also his privately-owned properties in the area, including his home abode, *Walmersley House*, lying close to the envisaged route of the railway line.

By way of background, John Robinson Kay's father Thomas Kay, owner of *Longholme Mills*, Rawtenstall, had bought him *Brooksbottoms Mill* (built in 1773) in Summerseat from Richard Hamer. Hamer's daughter Mary became Kay's wife in 1834, also to bring him Wood Road Mill on her father's death in 1850. A paternalistic employer, John Robinson Kay was to support the *Ten Hour Bill* of 1847 which looked to reduce hardship for workers by means of putting a cap on the daily number of hours having to be worked.

In the midst of the revolutionary new transport developments of the time, Kay sought to keep his hand on the tiller, influencing him to become a director of the East Lancashire Railway. In the event, both his business and residential property interests were to remain unscathed.

The Grants fight stubborn rearguard action

The section of line from Summerseat station onwards provided very challenging ground to engineer around and through, for one thing necessitating building a 400-yard (360m) long viaduct. A further short distance along the same line, a 423-yard (380m) tunnel also looked as it would have to be bored through solid rock in order to enable ELR trains to progress onwards to Ramsbottom.

In one sense, the Ashtons would have been satisfied by the fact that the railway route did not impinge on *Ramsbottom Mill* – likewise the Grants with regard to the *Square Works*. However, while the ELR seemed happy enough to leave the industrial premises of the town's leading mill-owners alone, a dilemma emerged though with regard to the Grant Brothers' private properties in the area. This included Daniel's *Springside Hall* residence -where elder brother William had also lived until passing away in 1842 - situated between Bury and Ramsbottom.

Another Grant brother, John, who was later to be described by the Grants' biographer, William Hume Elliot, as 'more of a yeoman than a merchant or manufacturer ' resided at the imposing *Nuttall Hall*, standing close to the *Square Works* on the other side of the banks of the River Irwell. This mansion was set in two acres of gardens, with woodland walks, ponds and waterfalls, features designed to add further to the idyllic, peaceful aura of the setting. Occupying the palatial *Nuttall Hall* with wife Elizabeth and children, John also had responsibility for the working operation of *Nuttall Mill* and the *Hall Farm*. [12]

Extensive landowners to the north of Bury, the Grants also became major shareholders in the railway company. This was to create a contentious situation all-round, particularly when the ELR announced that its proposed rail route from Bury through to Ramsbottom passed uncomfortably close to both *Springside* and *Nuttall* estates.

Daniel Grant subsequently became embroiled in a long-running dispute with the ELR Land Committee, the body bearing responsibility for having to resolve difficulties arising out of such issues. A series of negotiations ensued which had started with Daniel submitting a compensation claim for £5,000 just on account of the line being visible from his land. For its part, the ELR Land Committee at first only offered £2,000, which Daniel dismissed as a paltry sum. The amount offered was raised to £4,000 but not accepted. In the end, compromise was reached with Daniel settling for compensation at a rate which did not come cheaply for the company at £4,500 (the equivalent of over £500,000 in today's values).

Likewise John Grant was far from happy about the extent to which the line's route threatened the tranquillity of his *Nuttall Hall* estate. Displaying very much a NIMBY approach to the prospect of the hustle and bustle of railway presence despoiling the atmosphere of his grounds, the ELR felt obliged, at John's insistence, to undertake the building of the 115-yard (106m) *Nuttall Tunnel*, appeasing the squire's demand that his cherished view of the River Irwell should remain unsullied.

Furthermore, John was fastidious with regard to how the tunnel should look, demanding that it be castellated in a manner consistent with the architectural style of *Nuttall Hall Farm*. Certain distinctive features were incorporated into the tunnel's north entrance, including a coat of arms, a Lancashire rose, capped by a frieze decorated with seven carved, rather ghoulish-looking faces. This subsequently gave rise to speculation as to whether the faces were meant to represent those of directors of the East Lancashire Railway Company. [13]

The ELR looks to expand further

In the meantime, there was no shortage of other new projects to occupy the minds of ELR managers. During 1846, the company acquired the Liverpool, Ormskirk and Preston Railway (LO&PR), granting it direct access to the docks of the port of Liverpool. The LO&PR's line would run from a junction with the Liverpool and Bury Railway at Walton-on-the-Hill.

Following the acquisition on 3 August 1846, a disagreement ensued though when the ELR's proposal to build a new station at Preston, together with a separate line crossing the River Ribble, met with opposition from Preston Council who objected to the construction of a large extra commitment, including landscaping the embankment, creating an ornamental arch for carriages and pedestrians crossing under the railway, and building a footbridge on the river viaduct.

The ELR was learning quickly that, although gaining authorisation to build railway lines may have been a relatively straightforward matter at Parliamentary level, the process of translating plans into outcomes at the local level was fraught with complications. In that respect, the concerns of a whole range of different stake-holders had to be taken into account.

None of this though appeared to put a check on the company's vaulting ambitions to embark on further projects. Why in the heady atmosphere of the '*Railway Mania*' of the 1840s, when a whole host of start-up companies ploughed on ahead with profit margins uppermost in mind, would the ELR have reacted differently?

Notes

1. Martin Bairstow, 1993, *The East Lancashire Railway*, pub. Martin Bairstow, p. 5
2. Nigel Jepson, 2023, *The Railway Town of Ramsbottom*, pub. YouCaxton, p. 5
3. As item above p. 8
4. Minutes of Meeting of Provisional Committee of MB&RR, 29 September 1843
5. Nigel Jepson, *The Railway Town of Ramsbottom*, p. 9
6. See the author's publication *Ramsbottom's Revolutionary Doctor,* 2021, for more details regarding the Chartist movement, pub. YouCaxton
7. Nigel Jepson, Th*e Railway Town of Ramsbottom*, p. 11
8. *Manchester Guardian*, 26 September 1845
9. *Manchester Guardian*, 20 May 1846
10. John Francis, 1851, *History of the English Railway 1820-1845 Vol. II*, p. 69
11. Jeffrey Wells, 1995, *Railways In And Around Bury*, pub. Challenger, p.3
12. William Hume Elliot, 1906, *The Story of the "Cheeryble" Grants,* pub. Sherratt and Hughes, p. 122
13. Nigel Jepson, *The Railway Town of Ramsbottom*, p. 15

Chapter Three – Flags fly on the Bury-Rawtenstall line

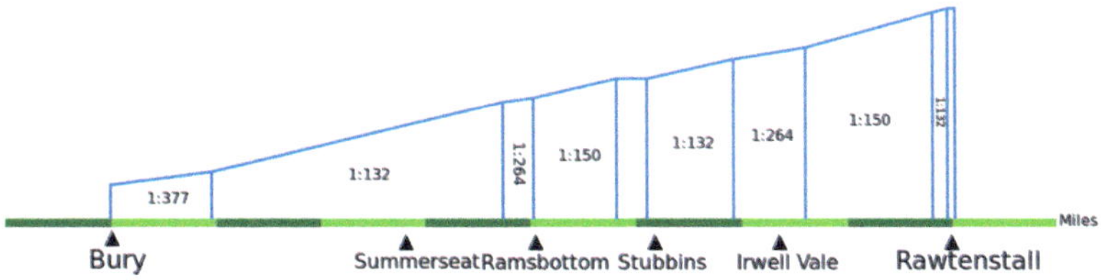

Bury to Rawtenstall Gradient Profile

Approval given and invitations sent out

Events took a very positive turn for the ELR during the latter half of 1846. It was announced that the 14-mile stretch of line between Clifton and Rawtenstall route was ready to be surveyed on behalf of the Board of Trade by the national Inspector-General of Railways, Sir Charles Pasley. Following his inspection on 23 September 1846, Pasley had given the final go-ahead for the service to commence operation. He was reported to have been 'very highly pleased with the good substantial character of the works'.

Since the original meeting of Bury and Rossendale businessmen at the *Red Lion*, it seemed a remarkably short time, only three years, before the project was completed and came into active operation. The advent of the railway was undoubtedly set to transform lives and livelihoods within the Bury and Rossendale communities it ran through.

Meanwhile, upwards of 1,000 invitations had already been sent out to company officials, shareholders and other local citizens in anticipation of the first journey along the line set to take place on Friday 25 September, only two days after Pasley's official authorisation. The conventional procedure was to run a celebratory 'special service' before the line was opened to the broader public. So it was that many of the invited guests gathered at Manchester Victoria station on Hunt's Bank on the Friday. *Bradshaw's Railway Gazette* remarked upon a distinguished number of people waiting on the platform including 'C. Nicholson, Esq, first managing director of the East Lancashire Railway'.

From those who had been present at that inaugural meeting held at the *Red Lion* in September 1843, John Robinson Kay, Thomas Aitken, Thomas Wrigley and John Grundy – who had become chairman of the board of directors by this time – were also noted as present, as were members of the Ashton family of Ramsbottom. No doubt Rawtenstall manufacturers – such as Henry Hoyle Hardman and David Whitehead – chose to put in their appearance at a point further down the line.

The train left Victoria station at twenty minutes past twelve o'clock, consisting of twenty carriages, drawn by the new and powerful steam-engine the *'Irwell'*, which was profusely decorated with small flags. A second locomotive was attached at Clifton Junction, at which stage the train ran onto the East Lancashire Railway itself. This was the point at which, as described earlier, several engineering feats had had to be carried out. Clifton Viaduct, consisting of thirteen stone arches, carried the line over the Irwell Valley.

Another crossing of the Irwell took place near Radcliffe. Throughout the populous village of Radcliffe the day had been declared a general holiday, and thousands of people were awaiting the arrival of the train. The bridges, fields, and embankments were covered with thousands of spectators, and from several heights in the neighbourhood flags and union jacks were waved.

Arriving in Bury at 1.15, the train service had the honour of being the first ever to enter the town. Halting there, the services of a third engine were enlisted and a further batch of coaches added. The experience of arriving in Bury was far from edifying in other ways though. Passengers found themselves in the middle of a huge building-site given that Bolton Street station was still in the throes of construction. However, this did nothing to dampen the spirits of all those caught up in the excitement of participating in the opening of this long-awaited stretch of new railway.

Inaugural train heads towards Ramsbottom

From Bury onwards, the number of coach carriages, painted sky blue and bearing the company's coat of arms, had grown to thirty-three in total. Lifting the atmosphere further, the 5th *Regiment of Foot* military band played popular tunes of the day for the benefit of the distinguished throng of passengers.

Just beyond Summerseat station, the train was carried over the River Irwell by a 400-yard long viaduct of eleven arches adjacent to the works of John Robinson Kay before disappearing in quick succession into the Brooksbottom and Nuttall tunnels. Emerging back out into daylight, passengers quickly caught sight of *Grants' Tower*, standing prominently on the skyline of the high ridge to the right, a four-storey construction built by the Grant Brothers in honour of their deceased parents William and Grace on the brow of the so-called '*Top o' th' Hoof*', high above the road connecting Bury and the upper reaches of Ramsbottom.

Crossing the Irwell again, this time over a trussed timber bridge, the line was carried over reservoirs by a viaduct of iron girders on stone piers before arriving, four miles down the line from Bury, at Ramsbottom with a sight of the Grant Brothers' *Square Works* to the left of the line.

From this point as far as Stubbins Bridge, the line was borne on a mile-long embankment before tackling the last more level stretch of the outward journey. With a palpable air of celebration, the special train eventually reached Rawtenstall station having taken thirty minutes to get there from Bury.

Shortly after the arrival of the train, about five hundred ladies and gentlemen sat down to a sumptuous 'collation' in one of the immense power-loom sheds in the works of J. Robinson Kay, Esq. John Grundy Esq. presided and J. Robinson Kay, Esq. occupied the vice-chair.

'Guests listened to several celebratory speeches, including one very lengthy one from managing director Cornelius Nicholson. A stranger to Bury and Rossendale, this ex-Mayor of Kendal had one thing in common with many in the community – he was a paper maker. In his spare time, he was also a freelance railway promoter who had been closely associated with the Lancashire & Carlisle and the Kendal & Windermere railways in their early days. 'On this occasion, he launched into a learned discourse on the *Forest of Rossendale*, which lasted for the best part of an hour.

'Three days later, on Monday 28 September 1846, the railway service opened to the public with a schedule of fourteen trains running daily between Salford and Bury in each direction, five of these reaching Ramsbottom and going on to Rawtenstall. Five trains travelled on Sundays. Facilities for goods traffic were to become available for use in 1847. [1]

§

ELR Locomotives

Using a variety of locomotives, the earliest the ELR put to work on the line were *2-2-2* engines of the Stephenson 'long boiler'-type and were built by Fenton, Craven and Company of Leeds in 1846. An order had been placed for twelve but in the event only four of the Leeds company's engines had actually been taken on, due to faults in construction. Richard Walker of Bury had also supplied four locomotives, *Medusa, Hecate, Diomed* and *Lynx*. These were later re-built as *2-4-0s* with enhanced cylinders and driving wheels. Other types of engine of the *2-2-2* wheel arrangement were to be used in following years, together with *2-4-0, 0-4-2* and *0-6-0* types.

Benefits of Rail Transport

From the very start, the railway was to prove most beneficial to the Bury and Rossendale area. For example, putting savings made by local businesses into context, the cost of transporting goods between Manchester and Rawtenstall by road in 1844 had been £1 and ½ pence per mile. In contrast, the maximum charges laid down under the new railway's tariffs were for 'road stone and agricultural materials 2d per ton per mile, foodstuffs 3 1/2 per ton per mile and for raw materials and manufactured goods 4d per ton per mile.'[2]

Enhanced speed of transport also brought great benefits. The existing 2½ hour length of time for a road journey between Manchester and Rawtenstall was reduced to less than an hour by rail. This had severe repercussions for road transport. The income of the Bury, Haslingden and Whalley turnpike, standing at £11,264 in 1845 fell to £8,283 in 1848, further plummeting to £4,892 by 1851.[3]

Two Bury stations open in the late 1840s

Although Bury Bolton Street station (at first it was just known as Bury station) was not actually completed until 23 August 1847, it was seen to have been worth the wait. Located below street level in a stone walled-lined cutting, a sloping driveway led down to platform level, east of the line. At the Bolton Street end, there were wrought iron gates bearing the crest of the ELR, with ornamental pillars. The station was designed to sumptuous specifications by the Manchester-based firm of architects, Messrs. Holden.

There were three platform faces. Two were on the island platform on the west side of the station. On the other (southbound) on the east side, was a three-storey Italianate building with a 60-yard frontage and 6-yard depth that contained normal station facilities but was also the head office of the ELR. It was brick-built with stone quoins and a hipped roof. On the ground floor, facing the platform, there were seventeen round-headed windows of the style the ELR favoured with more of the same on the first floor, and segmental arches above the windows on the upper storey.

By 1 May 1848, the town was able to boast two stations. This was because another line was set to open through Bury. The venture had been promoted by a group of East Lancashire industrialists who set up the Liverpool & Bury Railway (L&BR) as a means of gaining access to the port of Liverpool to bring in raw materials more effectively.

However, it hadn't been long before, by an Act of 27 July 1846, the L&BR had been absorbed into the Manchester and Leeds Railway (M&LR). On 9 July 1847, a further Act authorised the building of a line between Bury and Heywood which was an existing branch line (opened in 1841) connected to the M&LR main line at Castleton. The combined Acts had created a route between Rochdale (via Castleton) and Liverpool. Incidentally, as part of the 9 July Act, the M&LR, intent on further expansion, converted its name to the Lancashire & Yorkshire Railway (L&YR). Such were the swift interactions between different companies that were coming into play.

The Bury station, which served this line and had opened on 1 May 1848, was to become known in due course as Knowsley Street, to the south of the town centre. The L&YR line ran east/west through the town. The station had two platforms. A short distance to the west, the Manchester and Bury line of the ELR passed over the L&YR route. The north/south ELR line ran through the town at a similar elevation to the L&YR's but the Act authorising the Liverpool and Bury line had forbidden a flat crossing at Bury. For this reason, the L&YR line had to descend in order to pass under the ELR. This feature became known as the '*Bury Hollow*' or sometimes as the '*hump*'.

A link between the two systems, the Bury East Fork, opened at the same time as the route to Bolton on 20 November 1848. This steeply graded line branched off from the L&YR line on the west side of the Knowsley Street bridge, curving towards the north passing under Manchester Street after which it had its junction with the ELR. The link allowed through-trains of the two companies to run to and from destinations on their rival's routes.

Buckley Wells locomotive works

Based in Bury, Buckley Wells was where ELR locomotives were housed. Having overall responsibility for the site, Sylvester Lees had been appointed ELR's superintendent of the locomotive works from 1846 onwards. Meanwhile, James Newall had responsibility for the carriage and wagon section. His interest in mechanical engineering was to give rise to the invention of a braking system known as Newall's *Continual Brake*. This was applied to wagons and carriages and tested on the ELR. Between 15 September and 7 November 1853, an experimental train ran 5,874 miles without mishap.

An early Ordnance Survey map of Bury, surveyed in 1844 and published in 1851, points to the existence of an 'engine house' situated adjacent to the main line and to the south of the then-named Coal Pit Lane at Buckley Wells. Captain Tucker's O.S. map of 1846/7 also shows the same structure, thought to be a small timber 'engine house'. This building is considered to have been the ELR's original locomotive works. Although Company Board Minutes from these times indicate that existing facilities were never judged fit for purpose, it took until the mid-1850s for action to be taken to improve matters. John Shae Perring, the ELR engineer, drew up outline plans for a permanent locomotive, carriage and wagon works, making his submission to the ELR Directorate on 12 March 1855.

The *Manchester Guardian* of 22 September 1855 carried an advert in which the ELR invited tenders for the erection of locomotive workshops, boiler-makers' quarters, smithy, brass foundry, offices stores and engine house. One from James Hill of £6,600 was accepted. The extended Buckley Wells works, designed both to house and repair locomotives, opened during the summer of 1856.

Track Signals

Track signals employed in those early times were mainly of two types – station signals on posts, each post with two movable arms – and portable signals; flags were used by day, and coloured lanterns at night. The signals on posts were patented semaphore designs manufactured by Messrs. Stevens & Sons of the Darlington Works, Southwark. Each post had two arms – linked by chain to a foot control at the base – which were used to alert drivers on both the up and down lines. Each foot control was held in place by a hook on the post. An arm set at an angle would indicate that the train should approach slowly, before stopping at the station. The same arm set vertically would indicate that the train could pass through without stopping. The posts were also illuminated to allow use at night.

An interesting term arising from these early days was that of signalmen being called *bobbies*. The term *bobby* goes back to when local policemen were often called upon to carry out signalmen duties. The name was given to policemen in association with Sir Robert Peel, in his role as Home Secretary, who had created a new policing system after an Act passed in 1829.

ELR Stations

The ELR stations that were built during these times tended to emerge from one of three general 'models'. Bury Bolton Street, the principal station, as previously stated, was designed to very high specifications by the Manchester-based firm of architects Messrs. Holden.

Most other stations on ELR lines were based on a more modest template, designed by the company's engineer, John Shae Perring. Taking up post in the mid-1840s, whilst still only in his early 30s, Perring had had a somewhat unorthodox career path to date, his engineering skills having been employed in excavating Egyptian pyramids during the late 1830s, subsequently recording his findings in the three-volume *The Pyramids of Gizeh*, published between 1839 and 1842. Rather less monumental in scope than pyramids, Perring's stereotype ELR stations followed a somewhat more prosaic design, shaped out of stone and consisting of a station-master's room with an adjoining seated waiting area, ladies room and a booking office.

The third and cheapest design adopted the same general principles as above, only using brick and timber as materials. Other types of provision were still more basic. Summerseat for example, the next station down the line from Bury, was categorised in the ELR Guide as 'a roadside halt'. A driveway led up to the station building – 'consisting of no more than a wooden hut perched on the ground and a small goods yard comprising three sidings, a large goods shed with a 1.5 ton crane'. [4]

Ramsbottom station, opened on 25 September 1846, very much conformed to the standard Perring-style design described above. Double-track, its two platforms stood south of a level crossing at the bottom of Bridge Street. The main station building stood west of the line on the northbound platform. A stone-built goods shed was also put up west of the line.

Already providing an important link-point on this stretch of track, Ramsbottom Station was destined to grow in strategic significance with the later building of an ELR Extension Line to Accrington. It would require passengers travelling in that direction to have to change train at Ramsbottom, effectively taking Stubbins out of the equation. This was because Stubbins station (opened in January

1847) only had platform capacity to enable it to serve the through line to Rawtenstall. For some time thereafter, the station at Ramsbottom would be described on timetables as 'Ramsbottom Junction'.

Meanwhile, an intermediate stopping point between Stubbins and Rawtenstall lay at Ewood Bridge, a wayside station opened on 28 September 1846. It took its name from the village standing on the Edenfield to Haslingden Turnpike Road where the latter crossed the Irwell. The likely reason at the time for establishing a station here was to provide interchange between the railway and the road coaches which then plied between Accrington, Blackburn, Clitheroe and Whalley and towns to the south. This coach service was to be discontinued after the establishment of the ELR Accrington line in 1848.

Rawtenstall Station, in common with Ramsbottom and Ewood Bridge, had opened on 28 September 1846. It originally served as the single-line terminus for the Manchester-Bury-Rawtenstall line. The station was a grander affair enjoying the distinction, in common with Bolton Street Bury, of having been designed by Manchester-based architects Messrs. Holden. Most of its facilities were located on the 'Up' platform of the station (defined as such because trains standing at this platform headed 'up' towards the main station of Bury – despite it being a downward gradient!). These facilities consisted of one-storey stone-walled and slate-roofed buildings including waiting rooms, goods offices, inspector's office and the station master's house.

The ELR plan had always been to continue the line on to Bacup. Following an Act of Parliament passed on 27 July 1846, authorising the extension, it was inevitable that further work would need to be carried out to enhance facilities at Rawtenstall. As well as now having the authorised plan in hand to work on extending the Bury-Rawtenstall line to Bacup, an Act of Parliament had been passed on 3 August to build an ELR Extension Line to Accrington. At the very height now of '*Railway Mania*', no less than 263 Acts of Parliament had been passed in this single year setting up new lines.

As if embarking on two separate enterprises in the directions of Bacup and Accrington respectively was not enough, the ELR had also submitted proposals in November 1846 for a new line from

Buckley Wells (south of Bury) through Whitefield and Prestwich to Manchester Victoria Station. However, this other scheme was not to prove viable and progressed no further than the planning stage.

The ELR Accrington line: 1848

From the start, the ELR had perceived huge potential benefit from extending its existing line of communication to Accrington, not least for the purpose of connecting up to the Preston-Colne line to the north. Success did not come easily though in this venture. Several major engineering feats had to be negotiated in the process of laying a double track on a challenging steep upward incline which led to it being called the '*Alpine Line*'. From the junction at Stubbins, the route amounted to a 5-mile climb at an average gradient of 1 in 78 through Helmshore and Haslingden to a summit height of 771 feet above sea level at Baxenden.

Four different viaducts had to be constructed en route. The first, at Alderbottom, entailed a six span timber structure across the River Irwell just a short way downstream from a smaller wooden bridge on the Rawtenstall line. Both were later to be replaced by steel spans during the 1890s. The Irwell was re-crossed at Lumb by means of a stone viaduct of nine arches of 40 feet-span, 65 feet high, engineered by John Shae Perring and Sturges Meek. The three-span Ogden and seven-span Helmshore viaducts were followed by a bridge over the Haslingden Grane road consisting of wrought-iron tubular girders and with the tracks supported above on joists of timber and iron.

Reaching Helmshore, the level crossing at the south end of the station was the only one between Stubbins and Accrington. The line carried on beyond Helmshore along a seven-arch stone viaduct built on a curve south of Haslingden. Grane Road was crossed by twin wrought iron tubular grinders, later to be replaced by a plate girder bridge.

Athletic legend of James Edward ('*Choppy*') Warburton

Born in 1845 in Coal Hey, just off Lower Deardengate in Haslingden, '*Choppy*' Warburton was a famous local athlete who won more than

500 first prizes, including 75 cups, at events across the north of England. In all, he is said to have 'won more than 700 trophies, 511 before turning professional in 1880 at the age of 34. As a boy, he ran alongside steam trains on the local line, and was spotted by a wealthy local sports lover.' [5]

Remarkably, Warburton ended up in later life in Paris, having been hired to coach three up-and-coming cycling champions for the Simpson team based there: Jimmy Michael and the Linton brothers, Thomas and Arthur. Despite enjoying a degree of temporary success, all three died young from the effects of drug-taking. Although the practice was not illegal at that time, the premature deaths of all three of his charges in their 20's and 30's hardly reflected well on coach Warburton, who was eventually banned from the sport. *Choppy's* ill-fated sporting 'enterprise' did though gain some degree of immortality by being featured in a poster created by Henri de Toulouse-Lautrec, the famous French *art nouveau* artist of the time, designed to advertise and promote the team 'Choppy' Warburton was working for at the time, the Simpson chain company.

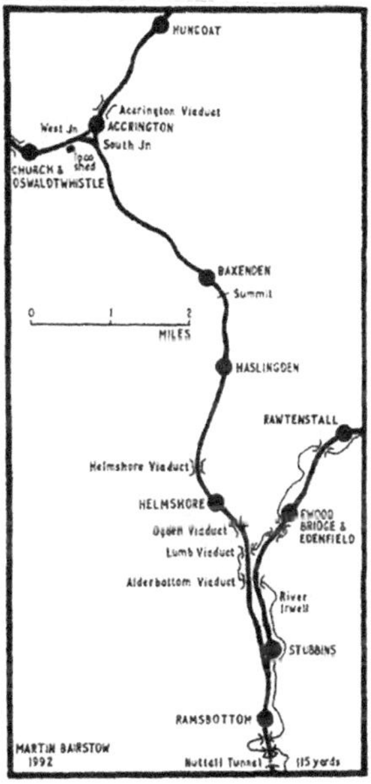

Ramsbottom to Accrington line

By way of attempting to explain the nickname *'Choppy'*, it was thought to have accrued on the back of his father's reputed occupation as a sailor regularly undertaking expeditions abroad. Whenever Warburton Senior had been asked what the weather conditions had been like on any of his voyages, he appears invariably to have answered: 'Choppy'. The credibility of Warburton Senior's status as a sailor is thrown somewhat into doubt though by the fact that, according to the UK census of 1871, he was categorised as 'a power-loom weaver in a cotton mill in Coal Hey, Haslingden'. It is thought that such a nose-to-the-grindstone job would have left him precious little scope for global navigation!

By way of postscript, on his own behalf, JE *'Choppy'* Warburton died of a heart attack in Wood Green, London, in 1897.

Continued rail journey from Helmshore to Accrington

A 146-yard tunnel led into Haslingden Station through which the line continued to climb until reaching a summit cutting which had been driven through difficult peat terrain. For three months, great masses of stone had to be sunk into the bog to drive out the water and obtain a firm foundation. There followed a descent at 1 in 100 through Baxenden Station, further steepening to 1 in 40 for most of the remaining two miles to Accrington. This was the notorious Baxenden Bank, known locally as the *Accrington Broo.* 'a veritable precipice shooting down to a villainous curve at the bottom, through Accrington Station where the speed limit was 5 mph.' [6]

Despite all the challenges that had been faced along the way, the 7½ mile line to Accrington was successfully opened on 17 August 1848 with the added dividend of opening up the rail network much wider. Situated at the junction between the Manchester, Preston and Colne lines, Accrington held an important position strategically. A glance at the 1849 timetable shows that seven trains per day ran on weekdays from Colne to Manchester with six running the other way. Stations were built along the line at Helmshore, Haslingden, Baxenden and Accrington. Accrington Station was described as 'a handsome building with a large four-dial clock on the centre of the roof, a public convenience which cannot fail to be highly-prized' [7]

However, in the event, it became known as one of the most inconvenient stations on the system. With only one platform, situated near the East Junction on the outside of the Colne to Manchester track, trains approaching the station from other directions had to be shunted to gain access to it. Further difficulties arose from the fact that whilst the main station building was sited adjacent to this platform, the booking office stood alongside the Preston to Colne track at the top of a footpath up from Blackburn Road. Meanwhile the engine and carriage sheds were placed in the middle of the triangular junction.

Not surprisingly in the circumstances, the station ended up having to be re-constructed in order to cope more adequately with all the new demands it had to face. Even so, it took until 1882 before the necessary work was carried out, entailing provision for four main platforms and two bays serving the Manchester to Colne as well as Preston to Colne tracks.

Single line from Rawtenstall to Newchurch: 1848

Authorisation for an extended line beyond Rawtenstall to Bacup had been enacted on 27 July 1846. A contract for building the line was agreed to in January 1847 with completion scheduled for December of the same year. Although it was to prove an impossibly optimistic plan of action, a single track did manage to be put into service on 27 March 1848 but only as far as the station at Newchurch. However, the project was fated to reach an impasse at this point. It would take another three years for further progress to be made from Newchurch towards the ultimate goal of reaching Bacup.

One notable side-effect of the ELR taking on the twin projects of extending its local network to both Accrington and Bacup was the consequence it had of reducing the 4-mile single line from Stubbins to Rawtenstall to branch line status. Trains heading on from the Bury end towards Accrington would pass through Stubbins Junction but without stopping at Stubbins station. From this time on, trains only stopped at Stubbins if headed for Rawtenstall.

Further Extensions

At this early stage of its existence, the ELR had every reason to be happy about its rate of development so far. As well as the stretch of line from Rawtenstall to Newchurch opening on 27 March 1848, there followed in June a Blackburn to Accrington connection (5.25 miles (8.45 km)) and in August, as already mentioned, the Stubbins to Accrington section. The line was extended east to Burnley (5.5 miles (8.9 km)) by September 1848 and, in February 1849, from Burnley to Colne, where it made an end-on junction with the Leeds and

Bradford Extension Railway, providing the ELR with a connection to Bradford and Leeds.

In financial terms, the ELR appeared to be accruing sound enough profit during these times. Taking 1847/8 as an indicator, the company reported in February 1848 an annual income for the previous twelve months of £553 18 shillings and 8 pence (£59,000 equivalent in 2022 values) for passengers and parcels and £498 10s 4d (£53,000 in 2022 values) for freight. Although these might not seem startlingly high profits, they were almost double those from the year before.

However, something of a post-*Railway Mania* recession was about to kick in which caused the company, like many others up and down the country, to adopt a more cautious approach by way of selecting which projects to push forward with and which to hold back on. For example, despite opening the line up to Newchurch, it was not until 1851 that work on the Rawtenstall to Bacup line was resumed. The scale and high cost of the engineering work entailed was a major factor in the delay.

Clifton Junction Blockade: **1849**

In the meantime, the ELR had found its attention diverted to a different kind of challenge altogether. On Monday 12 March 1849, a major dispute broke out between the ELR and the Lancashire and Yorkshire Railway (L&YR) which had led to 'a most extraordinary and unprecedented scene' at Clifton Junction.

The dispute arose from the fact that, with the ELR's line not starting until Clifton Junction, the company was constrained to pay the L&YR in order to operate its trains on their line from Clifton Junction to Manchester Victoria. However, an impasse was set to arise between the two companies regarding the method of collecting tolls for ELR passengers at the point at which they passed on to the L&YR line heading towards Manchester. Basically, it boiled down to the L&YR not trusting existing procedures and wanting to put things to the test.

The situation wasn't helped when the L&YR announced unilaterally that all trains should stop at Clifton to enable its company officers to count the number of passengers on board. The ELR, refusing to have such a system imposed on them, contended that existing practices of submitting returns should be maintained. Nor did it ease matters when the ELR alleged that the L&YR was only reacting like this out of spite because the ELR had recently won the right to connect up with Bradford and Leeds, having been in competition at the bidding stage with the L&YR.

Confrontation seemed inevitable when, during the week running up to 12 March, 'Blackmore, a L&YR officer, threatened to blockade the ELR who promptly issued a summons against him. Nevertheless, despite the presence of a large force of police, the threat was to be carried out.' [8]

On the Monday morning, L&YR managers ordered their platelayers to block the line with 'an immense baulk of timber' which was piled up high across the points prior to the first ELR train arriving on that morning. To strengthen the blockade, a L&YR train of six carriages was then backed up to the timber block. The plan was that passengers would be required to transfer from the ELR train under the terms that the L&YR was seeking to impose.

When the ELR train arrived on the Monday, L&YR ticket collectors boarded the carriages in an attempt to take tickets off passengers, but were unable to do so because the ELR had already taken these tickets off passengers at the previous station. However, the boarding of the train in this threatening manner: 'was the signal for retaliatory measures by the East Lancashire party, who had till now walked in silence on either side of their own line, as servants of the other company had done on theirs; the police meantime, looking on at both from their window of the railway station house. The first act of the East Lancashire Company's servants was to remove the baulk of timber, and this they did without hindrance; and the next to run forward their train and attempt to force before them the Lancashire and Yorkshire's blockading train. This however, the others appeared to have anticipated; and having put on the brakes and brought up another engine, they were able to maintain their ground.' [9]

Not to be outdone, the ELR officials ran a train of stone-filled wagons across the junction on the Up line, thus preventing all traffic between Manchester and Bolton. Scheduled trains now began to build up behind the blockade and soon eight were 'extended side by side for more than half a mile.' Many of the passengers got out to remonstrate with the railway officials and the police, who seemed most ineffective in dealing with situation. One group of passengers sent to Pendleton for a post-chaise, threatening to bring action for detention. After more than an hour, the Lancashire and Yorkshire blockading train was withdrawn and the East Lancashire travellers were allowed to complete their journey.

The matter was far from closed at this point though. The General Manager of the ELR, Richard Hacking, wrote to *The Times* newspaper expressing his annoyance at the L&YR's tactics. The so-called *Clifton Blockade* became serious enough to be raised in the House of Commons on 17 March. The case was eventually settled in court, with the ELR obliged thereafter to make a pro rata payment according to the distance travelled on each railway.

Inter-company disputes were far from infrequent. The ELR was involved in another in June of the following year, 1850, this time with the Bolton, Blackburn, Clitheroe and West Yorkshire Railway over running rights through Blackburn tunnel and station, ending up in its blockading of the line at Daisyfield for two days. More than 200 navvies, several engines and a heavy train of stone wagons were brought in and might have blocked the line for far longer had not the Lancashire and Yorkshire Company brought an end to the threatening impasse by making the question of the two companies' continuing access through to Salford one of joint self-interest to maintain.

Rawtenstall–Bacup line: 1852

Very soon after the incident had taken place at Clifton Junction in mid-March, thankfully better news was to arise for the ELR. On 2 April 1849, the LO&PR line to Lostock Hall (26 miles (42 km)) was completed and the (3 miles (4.8 km)) extension into Preston Station opened on 2 September 1850.

By September 1851, the project had resumed with regard to extending the ELR line from Rawtenstall as far as Bacup. On 29 September, five tenders had been received to carry out the remaining work. Predictably, given prevailing economic circumstances, the lowest tender at £27,845, that of Dickson & Mackenzie, Salop at almost £6,000 less than the next lowest of the five, was the one accepted.

For the price quoted, the winning contractors undertook to construct the necessary engineering work including boring three tunnels, carrying out all the civil works and laying the necessary track. The three tunnels that needed to be bored through were the so-called Newchurch No. 1, the Newchurch No. 2 and the Bacup tunnel at Stubbylee. Despite periods of strike action and inclement weather, the firm managed to achieve their objectives so that by 1 October 1852 the line was opened for rail passengers to travel through from Rawtenstall to Bacup, the station there achieving the status of being the highest station in the existing ELR network at 800 feet above sea level.

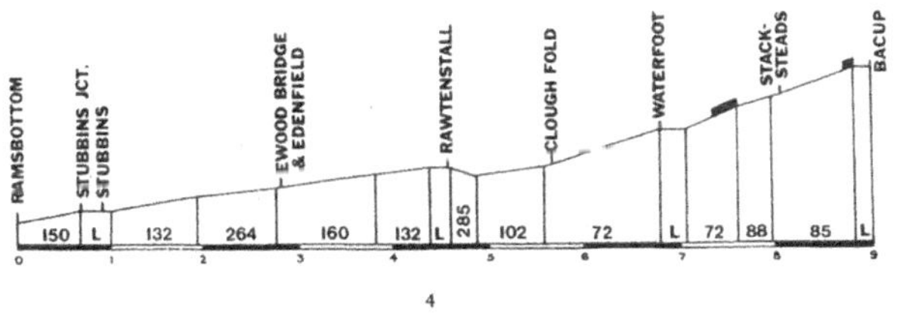

Ramsbottom to Bacup Gradient Profile

§

From those first pioneering meetings of Bury and Rossendale businessmen in 1843, less than a decade later an extensive rail network had been successfully carved out, not only connecting Bury and Rossendale with Manchester but to other places far and wide. The question now arose as to how far the rapid ELR progress made in the late 1840s might be successfully consolidated into the next decade.

Notes

1. Nigel Jepson, *The Railway Town of Ramsbottom*, pp. 19/20
2. MB&BR Act of 1844, pp. 105-6
3. Turnpike Statement and Accounts 1/26, 1848
4. Harrison & Sale's *Guide to the East Lancashire Railway*, 1849
5. Chris Aspin, *Private Letter*, November 2003
6. O.S. Nock, *The Lancashire & Yorkshire Railway – A Concise History*, p. 16
7. *Preston Guardian*: 19 August 1848
8. Geoffrey Holt, *A Regional History of the Railways of Great Britain Volume 10 – The North West*, pub. David and Charles 1978, p.168
9. Chris Aspin, *The First Industrial Society*, pp. 41-42

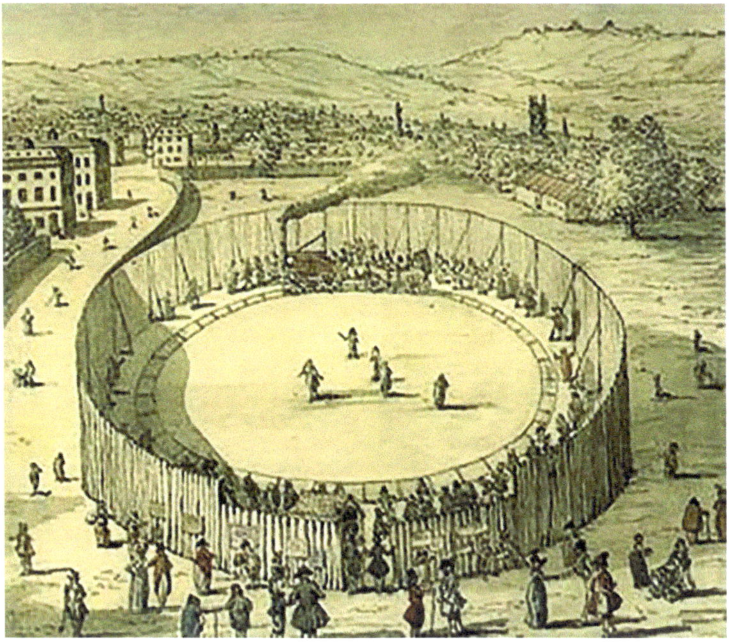

Trevithick's Catch Me Who Can

Rocket diagram

The Rocket National Railway Museum

Rocket carriages National Railway Museum

Stephenson's statue National Railway Museum

John Shae Perring1813-69 Egyptologist and rail engineer.

Bury Bolton Street station

Ramsbottom's original station.

Choppy Warburton's Team

Toulouse-Lautrec poster

Greenmount Railway station early Edwardian days

Annual Tradesmens Outing from Haslingden station c 1910

Goods Yard personnel at Bacup c1920s

Sir Nigel Gresley statue at Kings Cross station

Chapter Four – ELR goes out of existence in 1859

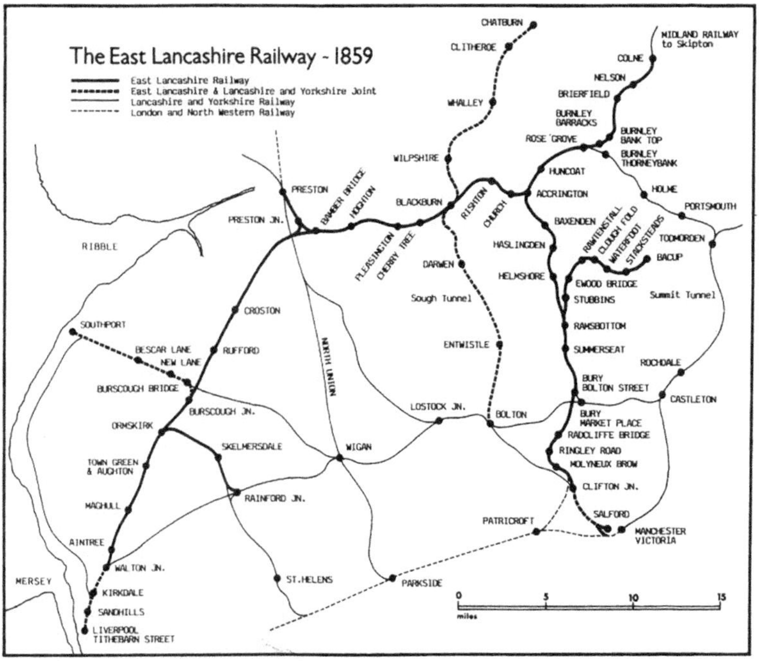

East Lancashire Railway-1859

Company rivalries continue

From the start of the 1840s, conflicts of interest inevitably arose between rival companies as competition become more intense. The ELR's main rival from the start had been the Lancashire & Yorkshire Railway. Antagonism had always simmered between the ELR and the L&YR but reached flashpoint in the '*Clifton Blockade*' episode of 12 March 1849. Although on the face of it, the matter had been resolved in a court settlement, the rivalry between the two companies persisted afterwards in a variety of guises.

For example, fierce competition centred upon the running of chartered trips to cities like Liverpool as well as the coastal resorts of Blackpool and Southport. Thanks to cheap rail fares though, large numbers of people visited the seaside who had never been able to do so before. At first, such outings usually went there and back on the same day. This was prior to arrangements like *Wakes Weeks* arising when all businesses in a town closed down for a week's holiday period.

Up to the late 1840s, it had been the custom though for mills or factories to allow workers only one or at most two days' holiday in the summer. Even so, such shortened outings never dispelled expectations of a thrilling experience, as conveyed in the following report in the *Blackburn Standard* of 6 June 1849: 'On Saturday morning last, soon after daybreak, many of the most active inhabitants of Helmshore and Haslingden were to be seen running backwards and forwards to call their more sleepy neighbours up, in order that they might not be late for the train which was to convey them to Liverpool and back. At five o'clock, both stations were thronged with lads and lasses in their 'very best' and there appeared to be a good sprinkling of men and women of more sober age...The Helmshore party consisted of a large number of work people in the employ of Messrs. W. & R. Turner, the extensive merchants at Helmshore, who came up to Haslingden in a long train of carriages drawn by three splendid engines at about seven o'clock. They had an excellent band of music with them, the performers being workmen in the employ of Messrs.Turner...Not a single accident happened during the day. On the return of the party, the police were in attendance to facilitate the careful emptying of the carriages'.

One of the passengers, then a boy of fourteen, recalled in later life: 'There were many stoppages on the way, but the novelty of the experience afforded compensation for a slow journey. At one point, there was a stoppage of over an hour and some of the trippers left the trucks, climbed the sloping embankment and went prospecting for drinks, the train restarting in their absence. The "carriages", he said, were open to wind and weather and the seats were far from comfortable by the end of the six-hour journey. One of the trippers declared that he could have reached Liverpool more quickly on a donkey.'[1]

Excursions Business

Considerable in-fighting broke out between railway companies following the opening of the Manchester-Southport line in 1855. This new route gave rise to an unprecedented level of competition regarding holiday traffic, provoking the following indignant outburst in a newspaper's leader column:

'The Lancashire and Yorkshire and the East Lancashire Railway are now running at an insane rate of competition which cannot end to the advantage of either company and which cannot much longer continue without entailing some unpleasant consequences on the public. The traffic competed for, is that between Manchester and intermediate stations of both lines, and Liverpool and Southport. To both these destinations passengers are conveyed at fabulously low prices and in number which call into exercise all the locomotive power of both companies. On Saturday last this absurd competition was brought to its culminating point by the conveyance of passengers from Manchester and Southport for one shilling – six miles for 1d. on one line and ten miles for 1d. on the other. Some 9,000 or 10,000 are said to have left Manchester on Saturday. Rough youths, frequently with tobacco pipes in their pockets, are thrust unceremoniously into first-class carriages. The effect of their occupancy of these vehicles may easily be conjectured. These cheap trips show the locomotive propensities of the masses.'[2]

Increasing competition between rival companies occurred in other arenas besides trips to coastal resorts. Every imaginable type of attraction seemed readily accessible now by the wondrous means of rail transport. On a cultural level for example, the ELR organised special trips for music lovers to Manchester, with great demand generated to go and see international stars such as the renowned soprano Jenny Lind (known as the '*Swedish Nightingale*') when she was engaged to sing at the Theatre Hall Manchester in 1847.

At the other end of good taste, Kirkdale Gaol, a few miles outside Liverpool, also became a popular attraction to go to by train. Since 1835, a number of public executions had taken place there, starting with that of John Barlow, of Bury, hanged for the crime of murdering his wife Priscilla. Up until 1848, the site had played host to eight more public hangings. Such spectacles, pandering to railway timetables by being scheduled to occur at midday, had generated audiences of more than 50,000 people by way of gratifying public demand.

Belle Vue Pleasure Gardens

Likewise, pleasure gardens became highly popular to visit via rail. The most famous of these newly-created northern pleasure grounds was *Belle Vue* in Manchester where one-time proprietor of the *Stockport Tea Gardens* John Jennison had transformed 36 acres of wasteland to create a highly attractive all-round experience for visitors. Opened in 1836, Jennison had capitalised on the closure of a private zoo in Higher Broughton, from which he had bought most of the stock he was able to put on show at *Belle Vue*. Through other sources though, he also managed to acquire star turns such as *The King of Oudh's Fighting Tiger* and a chimpanzee that smoked a pipe, drank tea and enjoyed being dressed as a swell. The zoo however was only one part of *Belle Vue's* portfolio of enticements. For example, as stated in Jennison's advertising material:

'The magnificent gardens constitute one of the most fashionable parades in the vicinity of Manchester... a labyrinth or maze on the same plan as the one at the Royal Gardens, Hampton Court...a fine bowling green...pleasure boats upon an extensive lake...wines, spirits and other refreshments may be had: and lunches, dinners and tea on reasonable terms.' [3]

Jennison also introduced horse and dog racing, a spectacular annual firework display - the first in 1852 was given the title of *The Bombardment of Algiers* - and the September brass band contest which began in 1853. One of the main problems in the early days for Belle Vue had been that of facilitating direct transport to the site. This had been overcome with the advent of railways and in particular the establishment from April 1843 onwards of a nearby station,

Longsight - featuring a giant platform, some 1,500 feet (457 metres) in length - which lay on the Manchester-Birmingham line. From this point on, all railway companies in the north-west, as well as many further afield, were able to provide services to this major attraction.

Tragic Accident at Helmshore: 1860

On 3 September, 1860, over 20,000 visitors had attended the annual brass band contest. Several trains had been commissioned by the L&YR railway company to take passengers to the site from towns including Blackburn, Accrington, Burnley, Colne, Haslingden and Helmshore. For passengers from Haslingden and Helmshore, three trains were put in place to convey them back home, the first setting off at 22.45pm, the second at 23.10pm and the third at 23.31pm. The first would carry 364 people to Ramsbottom before heading on towards Helmshore, then continuing to Accrington and surrounding areas.

The second train was also heading for Ramsbottom before making its way to Helmshore. Arriving there at 00.31am on Tuesday 4 September, although it coming to a standstill, a rebound of the carriages caused a screw coupling and two side chains to snap, resulting in up to 17 loose carriages beginning to move back down the line in the direction from which they had just come. The third train, having left Ramsbottom station, was on its way and passing the Ravenshore viaduct around 670 yards from Helmshore Station. Meanwhile, the loose carriages from the second train had begun to gain momentum on the 1-in-100 incline. In the darkness of the night, as the third train passed over the viaduct, the carriages smashed into the oncoming engine of train number three.

At least ten of the loose carriages were smashed to smithereens in the collision with 11 people dead and over a hundred passengers suffering severe injuries. Most of the casualties were from Accrington, Burnley, Barrowford and Colne. An Ewood Bridge man who was killed, Samuel Duckworth, was buried in St. James Churchyard, Haslingden. His gravestone reads: 'In Memory of SAMUEL DUCKWORTH of Ewood Bridge who was killed in the HELMSHORE RAILWAY ACCIDENT Sept. 4th 1860 in his 50th year. Sudden and awful was the stroke. By which lives thread was broke. Oh haste to Christ make no delay. As no one knows their dying day.' [4]

A Haslingden woman who also died in the accident was Mary Heys, daughter of James and Mary Heys of Mangholes, late of *Top o' the Bank*. She was buried in the family grave at Haslingden which reads: 'Mary their daughter was killed at the HELMSHORE RAILWAY ACCIDENT Sept. 4th 1860 51 years'...with the added citation: 'Oh death I little thought of thee, when I set out from home. But thy commission was for me. Oh what a sudden doom.'

Other 'Runaway Trains'

In the early years of railway development, due to lack of sufficient rigour in applying safety procedures, accidents were certainly not infrequent although thankfully never on the same scale as that which had occurred in September 1860. During Whitsuntide 1849, for example, a passenger train had been in a collision with an excursion train near Burnley. In January 1850, three people had died (reported in *The Times* on 8 January) when a luggage train ran into a passenger train at Maghull station. Another serious accident happened (reported in *The Times* on 22 October) at Clifton Junction on 19 October 1851 when a passenger train was derailed after passing the points on the junction, with several passengers seriously injured.

Owing to the steep gradient on the ELR line from Bury up to Rawtenstall, it was also not uncommon for 'runaway trains' to cause havoc during these early years. One such incident, based on a *Blackburn Standard* newspaper account, was described as follows on 28 December 1857: 'when a number of wagons laden with stone broke away from a train in Grane Road sidings, near Haslingden, and ran back down the incline towards Stubbins Junction three miles away. The guard, who had neglected to place pieces of timber between the spokes, jumped aboard the retreating wagons, but fell off near Helmshore Station'.

Catch points were not then in use; nor could anything be done to warn the driver of an oncoming passenger train of the runaway's approach. So violent was the collision that the last two carriages were uncoupled and began to move backwards. In one carriage were Mr.

Henry Hargreaves and his sister from Blackburn; in the other was a Mr. Littlewood.

Both men opened a door and, as the *Blackburn Standard* was to put it, 'Mr. Hargreaves asked Mr. Littlewood's opinion as to what was best to be done in the hope of effecting their escape. Mr. Littlewood shouted back that leaping out was their only hope. With the carriages rapidly gaining speed, Mr. Hargreaves took this advice and landed on the embankment, knocking himself out, but breaking no bones. Seeing her brother lying motionless by the track, Miss Hargreaves felt unable to follow. Mr. Littlewood also hesitated and it was not until the carriages had shot through Ramsbottom that he flung himself out and was seriously hurt. Miss Hargreaves, in the words of the subsequent report, 'was hurried on through tunnels until the impetus was exhausted, which was not before the carriages had nearly reached Bury'. [5]

The station master at Ramsbottom, 'who had seen the rapid transit of the carriages past his station, forthwith pursued them with a pilot engine and found Miss Hargreaves pacing backwards and forwards on the line near to a sawmill. He accommodated her with a seat on the tender and provided her with a covering as a protection from the rain, which was then copiously descending. Being thus made safe, she was conveyed on the tender back to Ramsbottom, where she found her brother anxiously awaiting her.' [6]

Given the thoroughly chaotic nature of events on that day, a major consolation in terms of outcomes was that it ended up being a lucky escape all round without loss of life or serious injury.

Continuing industrial growth in the Rossendale valley

By the 1840s, cotton had very much ousted wool as the mainstay of the Rossendale textiles industry, providing a variety of spinning, weaving and bleaching outlets. Added to this would emerge the felt industry, starting up in the 1850s and very quickly leading to the prosperous shoe and slipper (lending the area the name '*Slipper Valley*') specialism. Another main source of goods traffic was that of stone hewed from local quarries. This was much in demand to satisfy the building construction needs of burgeoning cities and towns throughout the north of England.

After the extension from Rawtenstall to Bacup was completed as a single line in October 1852, the increase in traffic in the mid-1850s had prompted double track provision to be laid down between Stubbins and Rawtenstall, operable from 15 July 1857 onwards. In addition to the existing Up platform at Rawtenstall, a *Down* platform was built. Connecting the platforms was a wrought iron foot-bridge which spanned the tracks at the eastern end of the station. Gas lamps were put up to provide light. It was not until 1876 though that authorisation was obtained for doubling the line through to Bacup itself.

The end of the ELR in 1859

In 1857, it might well have appeared to the general public that the ELR was still a growing business. The fact though was that it had always found itself struggling to compete against other better-financed companies. In basic terms, from 1850 onwards, the revenue taken by such as the L&YR and LNWR was respectively 5 and 15 times greater than that of the ELR.[7]

Even so, there had been something of a thaw in the relations between the ELR and the L&YR in recent times. For example, in order to avoid further unnecessary competition, the two companies had jointly taken over the Blackburn Railway in 1857. There had been two other occasions prior to this when a similar spirit of co-operation had prevailed. In 1854, an agreement had been reached on use of the Clifton Junction to Salford line. In 1855, the route between Burscough Bridge and Southport had been opened as a joint line between the companies. The last line to be operated as a purely ELR venture was a branch line from Ormskirk to Rainford Skelmersdale which opened on 1 March 1858.

Behind the scenes, discussions between the ELR and the L&YR had already started taking place with a view to a possible 'amalgamation'. Final terms were agreed by the start of 1859. However, there was some delay in obtaining parliamentary approval due to opposition to the scheme from the Midland and London & North Western Railways.

Ultimately, they were bought off and a Bill was finally passed on 13 August 1859. By this act, the ELR was dissolved and its capital of £3,448,397 united with that of the L&YR to make a total capital of £14,520,208.

Although it could be construed as a pooling of resources between the two companies, the arrangement unquestionably had the effect of bringing the existence of the ELR to an end, subsumed as it now was under the banner of the L&YR. However, it is interesting to note that, under the terms of the arrangement, the ex-ELR headquarters at Bury Bolton Street still remained in use in the same way as it had previously done. Whilst the L&YR's locomotive works were based at Miles Platting in Manchester, the ELR's own had always been at Buckley Wells in Bury. After 1859, Buckley Wells went on operating very much as it had done previously. Bearing this out, the L&YR maintained a distinct number list for locomotives in what became classified as the '*East Lancashire section*'.

Overall though, there must have been great sadness at the fact that the ELR title as a railway company in its own right was expunged from the records in 1859. It had achieved so much in a relatively short time but in the end fell victim to the fact that there were too many companies competing for the same business. "Survival of the fittest" was such that inevitably it was the financially weakest who would go to the wall. [8]

In personnel terms though, the L&YR didn't want to lose the expertise of key ex-ELR employees. For example, locomotive superintendent Sylvester Lees, who had been appointed to this position by the ELR back in 1846, was retained in office by the L&YR until his death on 22 March 1865. One-time Egyptologist John Shae Perring remained chief engineer of the ELR section until 4 July 1860 when the civil engineering department was concentrated in the hands of Sturges Meek, who had served the ELR before but been resident engineer with the L&YR since 1853. Perring was paid a year's salary up to 30 June 1861 and allowed to retire. He died at the age of 55 on 26 January 1869.

Despite the East Lancashire Railway going out of business in 1859, its legacy was assured in other ways. For example, all the lines it had put down during the course of its relatively short existence were set to continue functioning for the next hundred years and more.

Notes

1. Chris Aspin, *The First Industrial Society*, pp. 214-5
2. *Blackburn Standard*, 15 August 1855
3. *Zoological Gardens Brochure*, Belle Vue, Hyde Road, Manchester
4. Nigel Jepson, *The Railway Town of Ramsbottom*, pp. 34-5
5. *Blackburn Standard*, 29 September 1857
6. Chris Aspin, *Surprising Lancashire,* pub. *Helmshore Local History Society* 1988, pp. 40-1, based on a *Blackburn Standard* newspaper account of the incident
7. *Railway Times*, 1850, p. 659
8. Interestingly, the phrase "survival of the fittest" is thought to have been first coined by a 19th century economics theorist by the name of Herbert Spencer. It was more famously taken up by Charles Darwin in his ground-breaking book – *On the Origin of Species* – propounding the law of the "survival of the fittest" in his theory of evolution. Ironically, the first edition of his book had emerged in 1859, the same year as the original East Lancashire Railway went out of business. As if perhaps needless to say, there was no mention of railways in Darwin's book!

Chapter Five – L&YR extends operations

The Lancashire & Yorkshire Railway

The title 'Lancashire & Yorkshire Railway' had been adopted in 1847 and, with an amalgamation here and an acquisition there, it grew to be the main railway influence in most of Lancashire and a substantial force in the West Riding. It eventually covered almost 590 route miles and served 309 stations or halts...whilst its revenue in relation to its mileage was the greatest of any of the companies of the time.[1]

Locomotives of the L&YR were originally painted dark green with ornate brasswork and copper-plated chimneys. In 1876 the dark green was changed to light green and goods engines were painted black. The intensity of its services was reflected in the 1,650 locomotives it owned – it was by far the most densely-trafficked system in the British Isles with more locomotives per mile than any other company. [2]

Pattern and frequency of East Lancashire rail services - 1849 to 1880

In 1849, the ELR had provided eight trains each weekday from Salford to Bury together with two that started from Manchester Victoria. Six trains went on to Accrington. There were also six services to Newchurch, still at this time the terminus for the Rossendale line. Some of these involved a change of train at Ramsbottom. On Sundays there were five trains from Salford, three of which went through to Accrington and the other two to Newchurch. [3]

In 1855, by which time the single line had been opened to Bacup, there were eleven 'up' and ten 'down' trains daily with seven 'up' and eight 'down' on Sundays. 'Timetables show that the first and last two trains each day and all the Sunday trains were *"Government"* or *"Parliamentary"* trains which by law had to carry third-class passengers in covered vehicles.

By 1880, with provision of extra lines created in the meantime under the L&YR, the overall service became much more comprehensive. There were now three ways of getting from Bury to Manchester. The most prolific service was via Clifton Junction with 17 trains running each weekday.

Then there were 12 more via the recently-opened Prestwich route which had been opened on 1 September 1879 and provided an additional route to Manchester from Bury through rapidly developing residential areas. A similar number went via Heywood from Bury Market Place station (as Knowsley Street was called at this point in time). There were now 13 departures each weekday from Bury to Bacup, mostly coming through from Manchester via Prestwich. Also, there were 15 trains from Bury to Accrington, coming through from either Manchester Victoria or Salford via Clifton Junction. Sunday trains operated on all these routes but with much lower frequency.

Conversions at Ramsbottom, Summerseat, Stubbins and Ewood Bridge stations

By the late 1850s, Ramsbottom had grown quickly with many more factories opened. The L&YR started to use the route through Ramsbottom as a viable alternative to its existing congested main line between Manchester and Leeds, bringing much extra traffic.

During the early years of L&YR ownership, passenger train services had continued to run to Manchester via Clifton Junction but from 1 September 1879 passenger services that had originated from the Bacup line were transferred south of Bury from the route via Clifton Junction to the new line running via Prestwich. Meanwhile, Accrington trains continued to run via Clifton Junction.

In the 1880s, the L&YR decided it necessary to enhance facilities at Ramsbottom. By this time, there were 14 northbound weekday trains to Colne and the same number to Manchester Victoria. Work had begun in the 1880s on the establishment of a goods yard with sidings on both sides of the line running behind the two platforms. In 1875, a signal box had been installed on the north side of the level crossing, west of the line. This was supplemented by the later addition of a signal box on the Up side to the south of the station which controlled the sidings and goods yard. There were also two 'private' sidings. One of these served the bleaching works of Hepburn & Co. who in the mid-60s had taken over the site of the *Square Works* when the Grants' business had closed down.

After both remaining original 'Grant brothers', John and Daniel, had died in 1855, the family business had passed on to William and Robert Dalglish Grant, sons of John. Neither enjoyed good health though with Robert dying in 1863. William, at a time when the effects of the American Civil War brought about a 'cotton famine' and trade recession, had sold the business to Hepburn & Co.

The second of the two 'private' sidings referred to above, which were accessed by a turntable from the goods yard, served the *Ramsbottom Paper Mill* on the east side. Further alterations to the station included the construction in 1893 of a wooden footbridge, half-glazed and roofed, connecting up the two platforms at the level crossing end of the station. In terms of basic infrastructure, the station ended up being equipped with single-storey stone buildings on the Down platform, incorporating the main entrance, booking office, waiting rooms and staff facilities. A lengthy glazed canopy, of ridge and furrow design, extended from the north end of the platform for half the length of the station. On the southbound platform, single-storey brick and wooden buildings provided shelter for passengers and storage facilities for staff.

Later on in time, Ramsbottom Urban District Council introduced an electric trolley bus service which opened on 14 August 1913. It ran from *The Hare and Hounds* in Holcombe Brook to Market Place, Ramsbottom, and then on to Edenfield. Another service ran from Market Place to Ramsbottom station. However, this added leg was to prove short-lived being abandoned on 5 October 1914 soon after the outbreak of World War I. The service from Holcombe Brook to Edenfield went on running until closed on 31 March 1931.

Meanwhile in 1860, the L&YR had built a new station at Summerseat. Constructed out of sandstone, it was single-storey, with coupled round-headed windows (very much in Perring style) near each end of the platform elevation. In 1875, a wooden signal box was opened at the north end of the northbound platform, replacing the box on the southbound platform. In relation to Stubbins and Ewood Bridge stations, the original simple wooden buildings had been re-built in stone and included booking-offices, waiting rooms and a station master's house. Ewood Bridge, re-named Ewood Bridge & Edenfield in 1891, also had a siding with goods warehouse, weighing machine and crane. [4]

Bury – Holcombe Brook branch line: 1882

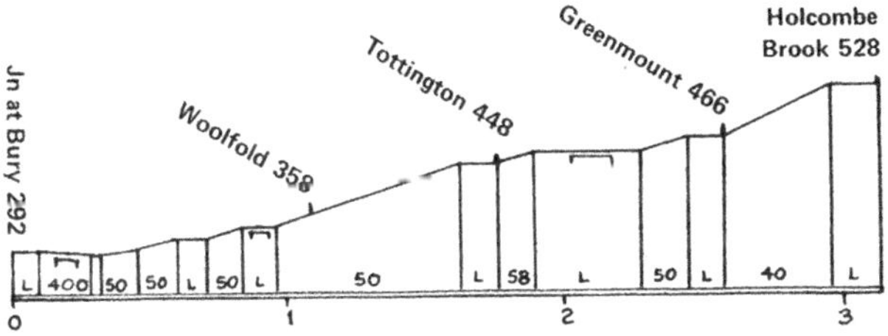

[4]

Bury to Holcombe Brook- Gradient Profile

A particularly significant new development, taking place in the early 1880s, was the opening of a branch line between Bury and Holcombe Brook. In the same way that Bury and Rossendale businessmen had lobbied for the construction of a railway, so in the 1870s manufacturers in the Tottington district pressed for a rail connection in order to prevent its district becoming an industrial backwater

Two of the prime movers behind the initiative were Richard Olive and Samuel Knowles. Born in 1837, Richard Olive was by the time of the 1881 census aged 43 and living with his wife and two children at the *Springside* property in Walmersley which had formerly been the residence of Grant brothers William and Daniel. He was the owner of a paper mill and wagon-making works, boasting a combined work-force of 500, in Woolfold in the Tottington area. Samuel Knowles was the younger step-brother of Joshua Knowles. In 1821, whilst still in his early 20s, Joshua had acquired *Tottington Mill.* He had extended the works so that by 1823, 300 people were employed there. By 1841, this had risen to 443, of whom 139 though were children under the age of 13.

Joshua had constructed *Tower Farm* on the edge of Greenmount in 1840. This distinctive edifice was modelled on John Grant's *Nuttall Hall Farm* (Joshua had once worked at the Grants' mill in Ramsbottom and admired all that the brothers accomplished) with its fifty square foot castellated water tower and row of arches round the top, replicating the tops of medieval fortifications. The practical consideration behind building *Tower Farm* had been to stable the many heavy horses required during those times to convey coal from Affetside as well as transporting raw materials, and finished goods from *Tottington Mill* to Bury and elsewhere.

Following the death of Joshua in 1853, Samuel came to inherit his elder step-brother's various properties. It was in the middle years of the 1870s that Samuel, aware that the days of reliance on horse-and-cart transport were well and truly over, took it upon himself to form a railway company along with three other manufacturers in the area: Richard Olive of *Woolfold*, Edward Mucklow of *Elton Fold* and Hugh Roberts of *Stormer Hill.*

In 1876, the Bury and Tottington Railway Company had been formed with the aim of building a line stretching from Bury to Holcombe Brook. An Act of Parliament was passed on 2 August 1877 authorising the construction of the railway with added provision to incorporate a subsidiary line from Woolfold westwards to serve Richard Olive's wagon works.

It took four years until 6 November 1882 though before the line was opened for passenger and freight traffic. This was because of the many engineering exercises needing to be carried out, for example three viaducts. The first, comprising five skew arches built in stone, carried the line over the River Irwell shortly after leaving *Tottington Junction.* Another five-arch structure crossed the Kirklees Brook just before the station at Woolfold. Between Tottington and Greenmount, the largest viaduct crossed *Scholes Lodge* by means of nine arches. Out of Bury, the route climbed at a gradient of 1:50 most of the way, stepping up to 1:40 over the final mile.

Across the 3.75 mile length of track, there were various scheduled stops at Woodhill, Brandlesholme, Olive's, Woolfold, Sunnywood, Tottington, Knowles, Greenmount and Holcombe Brook. However, several of these stops were so-called 'halts' rather than stations, lacking proper platforms, instead relying on retractable steps being fitted to carriages to allow passengers to board and alight.

To celebrate the opening on 6 November 1882, Samuel Knowles and Hugh Roberts paid for all their employees to go on a day-trip to *Belle Vue Gardens* in Manchester. More conventional local services operated soon afterwards, consisting of a timetable of six midweek return trains running from Bury Bolton Street to Holcombe Brook, which were driven by L&YR steam engines. A working agreement between the BTDR and the L&YR granted the latter company 54% of the traffic receipts in return for the use of L&YR locomotive power and rolling stock.

Freight receipts were set to exceed those from the passenger side of the service by about a double amount. For example, passenger receipts in 1883 were £1,496 compared with freight at £2,855. In 1884, the figures were £1,352 and £2,822 respectively. Even though the BTDR branch line might have benefitted from the growing popularity of Holcombe Brook, based on proximity to *Peel Monument*, it had to compete with the L&YR's alternative stations at Ramsbottom and Summerseat, also conveniently situated for reaching the *Monument*. In addition, the branch line suffered from road competition, the steam tramway service between Bury and Tottington beginning in 1883.

"Survival of the fittest" applied in the end with the BTDR in effect coming to an end as the result of an act of Parliament passed on 24 July 1888 after just less than six years of operation. From this time on, the L&YR took over full control of the branch line.

Bacup becomes a railway hub

Work had finally started in 1878 to lay a double track between Rawtenstall and Bacup. It necessitated another single line tunnel being built at Newchurch, 592 yards in length, in order to accommodate the westbound Up line. It had been intended to call this tunnel Newchurch No. 3 but instead it was to be known as *Thrutch Tunnel* by the men who bored it, and that became the official name. *'Thrutch'* in local dialect was a verb used to describe the process of blasting and boring through solid rock.

During the widening of the line, the intermediate stations at Clough Fold, Newchurch and Stacksteads were altered to conform to double line standards. 'Newchurch' was re-named 'Waterfoot for Newchurch'. The double L&YR line through from Rawtenstall to Bacup was completed and ready for inspection by the Board of Trade on 9 March 1881, the exercise undertaken by Major-General Charles Hutchinson, noted for his work in connection with the Tay and Forth bridges in Scotland.

The completion of the double line from Rawtenstall coincided with the opening of a line connecting Bacup up with Rochdale in the other direction. The two-way process entailed remodelling and enlarging Bacup station in readiness for it to take traffic from either direction. The line's first public service began shortly afterwards on 17 March 1881 although the newly-enlarged Bacup station was not officially opened until rather later. On 4 June, the *Bacup Times* proudly informed its readers: 'The various works at our new station at Bacup are now approaching completion...Bacup will then be able to boast one of the neatest stations to be found on the lines of the Lancashire and Yorkshire Railway'. [5]

Facilities consisted of a wide island platform with a track on either side, each with an engine-releasing loop. A single-storey brick building containing the booking hall and a lamp room stood at the north end of the station. A substantial awning extended about two-thirds of the length of the platform and two waiting rooms were installed beneath it. Goods facilities of the redeveloped station comprised sidings and a large goods shed. A station signal box was constructed in 1892.

Changes to Bury Bolton Street station in 1883

The L&YR also made it a priority to update provision at Bury Bolton Street station at this stage. Work on this project was completed in

1883 as the *Manchester Guardian* article of 12 May 1883 describes: 'The Lancashire and Yorkshire Railway Company have almost completed a new station at Bury at a cost of from £10,000 to £12,000. The platforms have been raised and lengthened and now extend 250 yards. On the *Down* island platform are new waiting rooms. The new station is carried over the line and faces Bolton Street, being set back to all carriages to put down passengers at the door of the Booking Office. The passengers descend by a covered approach to an overbridge, which leads to either platform without the necessity of crossing the lines as before. The approach and overbridge are roofed in and glazed and the station and approaches are lighted with Bray's lamps. The works have been carried out by Mr. Charles Brierley, builder, Bury.' [6]

Access to the station was via the main booking office on Bolton Street, this office standing on the left of the booking hall, with a *WH Smith* bookstall on the right. An alternative entrance could be made by way of a sloping driveway down to a set of iron gates, beyond which lay a ticket collector's cabin guarding a small side entrance to the *Up* platform. Amenities on the ground floor of the old ELR building were provided for both passengers and staff. These included waiting rooms, rest rooms, urinals, parcel office, telegraph office, guards' room, stores, porters' room and station master's office.

During the 1860s, the Buckley Wells locomotive works had been extended, suiting the needs of the L&YR. Further alteration took place in the 1870s with the construction of an engine shed on the west side completed in 1876. With a company decision though to make a move to Horwich in 1888, locomotive repair was subsequently to be carried out there, leaving Buckley Wells largely confined to carriage repair and maintenance.

As previously mentioned, *Bury East Fork* was an early provision which allowed trains to intersect across east/west and north/south routes. Work now had started to take place with regard to the *Bury Loop*. Longer and of lesser curvature and gradient, work had begun in 1898 and involved a 70 yards-long covered way beneath both Manchester Old and New Roads. *The Loop* was inspected by the Board of Trade and opened for traffic on 11 July 1899. It connected the east-west route at Bury Loop Junction with the Clifton to Accrington line at Bury Loco Junction, south of Buckley Wells.

The Newton Heath L&YR Football Club

An unlikely sounding chapter in the broader social history of the L&YR was to arise in 1878 following the formation of a notably successful in-house football club by the name of *Newton Heath LYR*. It was centred on the Carriage and Wagon department of the Lancashire and Yorkshire depot at Newton Heath in Manchester. The team initially played games against other departments and rail companies. On 20 November 1880, they widened their compass by taking on Bolton Wanderers' reserve team, a match though which they lost 6-0.

Up until 1893, Newton Heath played on a field on North Road, close to the railway yard. Although playing in a variety of strips, their favoured colours were the green and gold colours of the railway company. The highest attendance during this early period was an estimated 15,000 for a friendly match against *Gorton Villa* on 5 September 1888. In that same year, the club had become a founding member of *The Combination*, a leading regional football league.

Following the dissolution of *The Combination* after only one season, Newton Heath joined the newly-formed *Football Alliance*, which ran for three seasons before being merged with the *Football League*. At the start of the 1892/3 season, the club was playing in the exalted realms of the *First Division* of the *Football League*. Although many of those playing for the team were still working as railway employees, the club looked to broaden its horizons and asserted its independence from the railway company, dropping the L&YR from its name and at the same time moving to new ground premises at Bank Street.

One particular player who enjoyed particular success at the club, both on and off the field, was Harry Stafford. Born in Crewe in 1869, he worked for the London and North Western Railway (LNWR) as a locomotive boilermaker at the Crewe works. A talented footballer, he had made his debut for *Crewe Alexandra Hornets* at the age of 22 and went on to make over 80 appearances for the club before in 1896 moving on to play professionally for the *Newton Heath Heathens*.

First-choice right back and captain of the team, making 184 appearances between 1896 and 1903, Harry Stafford was also to be remembered in club history for the financial backing he won for the club at a perilous time in its fortunes. In January 1902, with debts amassing of £2,670 - equivalent to £310,000 nowadays - the club had been served a winding-up order. Taking it upon himself to seek sponsorship from local businessmen, he was successful in his approach to John Henry Davies, a wealthy brewery owner. Davies later became club president and, apart from financial investment, was influential in the club's name being changed to *Manchester United* in 1902.

Starting off in the Second Division, the newly-named club gained promotion in 1906 and won the *First Division* championship in 1908. With John Henry Davies continuing to pump money into the club, a decision was taken to move from Bank Street to a new ground offering extra crowd capacity. In February 1909, six weeks before the club won its first FA Cup title, *Old Trafford* was named as the new home of *Manchester United*, following the purchase of land for around £60,000.

A curious twist of fate was to occur a century later when a splinter-group of disaffected *Manchester United* fans created a new club, *FC United of Manchester*, which sought to re-kindle the less commercialised spirit of those former Newton Heath-associated times.

Railmotors and electrification on the Holcombe Brook branch line

Since taking over the Bury/Holcombe Brook branch line in 1888, the L&YR had not had things all its own way in running the business. First there had been competition from steam-hauled trams operating from Bury to Tottington. The problem was exacerbated in 1904 with the added rivalry of Bury Corporation's electric trams which travelled over the same route. In response, the L&YR looked to meet the challenge, resorting to latest technological advances, by way of installing railmotors in 1905. These pioneering railmotors, manufactured by Kerr, Stuart & Co. of Preston, comprised: 'an articulated unit of steam motor and carriage, the steam motor having the characteristics of two transverse boilers and three smokebox doors.' [7]

However, it was found that the units were under-powered for the purpose of climbing the steep branch-line gradient and were subsequently replaced by Horwich-built railmotors which proved more powerful. From the late 1880s onwards, Horwich, near Bolton, had become the new site of the L&YR's own locomotive works, replacing Miles Platting in Manchester. The switch in April 1884 had involved a £36,000 purchase of 350 acres of land. This new complex, designed by experienced railway engineer John Ramsbottom, was modelled on a similar system operating at the *Crewe Works* in Cheshire.

Further development came in the form of an approach made in 1912 to the L&YR by Dick, Kerr & Co. (the brand name largely following on from its predecessor company Kerr, Stuart & Co.) offering at its own expense to trial a high-voltage experimentation on the Holcombe Brook line. At the time, the Preston firm, having its eyes on a lucrative electrification deal in Brazil, was looking to test things out somewhere more local. The result was that the Holcombe Brook line enjoyed the distinction of being one of the first high-voltage railways in the world.

Work on the scheme involved positioning overhead gantries between Bolton Street station and Tottington Junction with single 'tram' masts needing to be placed on the east side of the line. The first fare-paying service began on 29 July 1913. The pioneering scheme was described in the following way: 'The very interesting experimental line equipped by the L&YR for 3,500 volts continuous current, working between Bury and Holcombe Brook, has two motors on its motor coaches permanently in series, and a generator for providing current at 100 volts for the auxiliary service of control, brake pump lighting and heating.' [8]

Including gradients of 1 in 50 and 1 in 40, and from the way the pioneer electric locomotive quietly, but not very rapidly, climbed these gradients it became known as the *Beetle*. [9]

'Little Billie'

In 1914, the L&YR introduced a 'Rail-motor' service – to become known affectionately as *Little Billie* – between Ramsbottom and Bacup, calling off at all stations and supplementing trains that ran through to Manchester. The L&YR pressed ahead with electrification between Bury Bolton Street and Manchester Victoria via Prestwich. A frequent service of electric trains began on the Prestwich route on 17 April 1916. It proved very popular, passenger journeys increasing from 1,884,776 in 1907 to 2,518,638 by the end of 1916.

Meanwhile Bacup line trains were diverted via Bury Knowsley Street and Heywood as soon as the electric services began. This added a considerable mileage to their route but it was assumed that most passengers from Bacup line stations to Manchester would change onto the electric services at Bury Bolton Street.

Outbreak of World War One: 1914

The conflagration that started in 1914 was set to last through until 1918. Inevitably, it meant that local matters paled into insignificance by comparison with the scale of challenge facing the nation of fighting a war abroad. With railways coming under state control, the immediate challenge lay in terms of transporting troops, horses, military equipment and medical supplies to ports facing Europe.

Although it was to be a war that was largely fought abroad, for people living in Rossendale the night of 25 September 1916 was to be remembered for an air offensive on a serious scale. This happened after a huge Zeppelin airship (entering the country over the Lincolnshire coast) threatened Rossendale on the night. The first damage of significance occurred when a salvo of five explosive and two incendiary bombs were dropped at Ewood Bridge resulting in a section of rail track being destroyed just north of Irwell Vale Bridge.

After passing over Helmshore, *Zeppelin L21,* commanded by Oberleutnant Kurt Frankenberg of the Imperial German Navy, dropped five more bombs on Holcombe on its way to Bolton. As well as Holcombe Post Office suffering damage, the *Shoulder of Mutton* public house had twenty of its windows shattered and the front door broken in half. A further bomb fell by the gable (Helmshore end) of

Holcombe School, causing severe damage, also breaking the church clock and smashing windows. The only casualty of this part of the raid happened in fact to be a thrush, the body of which was preserved by a taxidermist: thereafter kept on exhibit in a glass case on school premises.

It was thought that the Zeppelin pilot's original target had been industrial Manchester but that in an atmosphere of mounting confusion, uncertain about directions, bombs were randomly discharged over any built-up areas that happened to come into view from aloft. While there were no human casualties in Rossendale, the civilian death toll in Bolton was to reach thirteen, 'made up of five men, five women and three young girls aged seventeen, five and two'.[10]

By way of postscript, just over two months later, in the early morning of 28 November 1916, 29-year old Frankenberg and his L21 were shot down in flames, after carrying out a raid in West Yorkshire and the Staffordshire Pottery Towns, by a British plane off the east coast, near to Lowestoft.

Wider effects of the war

The challenge of keeping the domestic rail system operating during these critical times was logistically compounded by the fact that 100,000 male rail workers were enlisted as soldiers and went to fight abroad. Before the war, an estimated number of 13,000 women had been working on the railway, mostly carrying out domestic duties such as cleaning and washing. Soon after the beginning of World War I, the number had increased to 70,000 with women taking up a wide range of roles, including higher order roles such as engineering.

Many firms, such as the Preston firm of Dick, Kerrs, that had previously been specialist transport operators, now found themselves diverting to war-based operations such as munitions manufacture, principally involving women workers. From June 1915 onwards, around 2,200 shells were made every week.

Extra enthusiasm to support the war effort generated itself in other ways, for example playing football matches with gate-money being donated to war charities. As a 'Ladies football team', *Dick, Kerrs* enjoyed outstanding success with the team's matches attracting anywhere from 4,000 to over 50,000 spectators a match. In 1920, *Dick, Kerr Ladies*, representing England, defeated a side representing France 2-0 in front of 25,000 people, a game that went down in history as the first international women's association football game. [11]

All such participation seemed very much a 'roller coaster' at the time with no questions asked while war was being waged. However, on cessation of war, the continued existence of the team encountered strong opposition from the *Football Association*. Following the resumption of the normal football programme for men, the FA took the action in 1921 of banning women from using fields and stadia controlled by FA-affiliated clubs. The ban was to stay in place for all of fifty years, not being finally rescinded until 1971.

The same outcome arose as far as women railway workers were concerned. The skilled jobs which they had carried out during wartime largely reverted to men on de-mob.

Post-World War 1 rationalisation of the Railway System

At the time of the outbreak of World War I in 1914, there had been as many as 120 separate railway companies operating across Britain. This was seen as far too many and that economics of scale should be made by adopting a more coherent approach to running the rail network. Following the end of hostilities in 1918, the ruling coalition government under Prime Minister Lloyd George had passed a *Railway Act* reducing down to four larger regional entities. The so-called *Big Four* consisted of the Great Western Railway (GWR), the London, Midland & Scottish Railway (LMS), the London & North Eastern Railway (LNER) and the Southern Railway (SR).From this time onwards, the hitherto L&YR-controlled lines in East Lancashire were absorbed under the banner of the London, Midland & Scottish (LMS).

Notes

1. Michael Blakemore, *The Lancashire & Yorkshire Railway* p. 5
2. *The Railway Publishing Company Ltd.*, 1920, p. 168
3. Nigel Jepson, *The Railway Town of Ramsbottom*, p. 37
4. As item above, pp. 39-40

5. *Bacup Times*, 4 June 1881
6. *Manchester Guardian*, 12 May 1883
7. Jeffrey Wells, *Railways In And Around Bury, p.79*
8. *Railway News*, 21 February 1914
9. O.S. Nock, *The Lancashire & Yorkshire Railway – A Concise History* p. 139
10. Peter JC Smith, 1991, *Zeppelins over Lancashire* pub. Neil Richardson p.20
11. Gail J Newsham, 2018, *In A League Of Their Own* pub. Lightning Source UK Ltd., pp. 58-63

Chapter Six – Long decline of rail transport up to the 1960s

Train Services across East Lancashire during the inter-war period

By 1932, passengers using Bury Bolton Street station had the choice of three separate routes to Manchester Victoria, services to Accrington, Bacup, Burnley, Colne and Holcombe Brook as well as shorter workings to Bury Knowsley Street and Ramsbottom stations.

In all, there were 99 weekday southbound departures from Bolton Street. The majority were electrics on the Prestwich route. These ran at least every twenty minutes for most of the day. The first southbound train left at 5.15 am for Manchester Victoria. The last southbound service departed at 11.10 pm for Manchester. Going northbound, there were 68 trains. 29 of these were on the electric service to Holcombe Brook. Of the remainder, 21 went to Bacup with the rest taking the Accrington route and most of them going to Colne. The first northbound train left for Stubbins at 5.30 am. The last was for Bacup and departed at 11.17 pm.

Excursions and *Wakes Weeks*

In addition to the trains listed on the day-to-day public timetable, there were the excursion and holiday trains. When holidays with pay became much more the norm after the First World War, the practice was for each town to hold a '*Wakes Week*' with most employers shutting down their works for the week.

Margaret Ferguson, a child living in Ramsbottom at the time, was later to recall: 'I should think that at least 90% of the local population went on holiday in the annual *Wakes Weeks*, mostly to Blackpool, or St. Anne's if you were slightly more posh, whilst the really posh went to Colwyn Bay, Rhyl or Llandudno...The whole of Ramsbottom seemed to shut down, every mill, every shop, no papers, no bread, no nothing!

'My Dad being a railway employee was allowed a certain number of free passes every year...Sometimes Mam would take me to Blackpool for the day and arrangements were made to see Aunt Alice and Uncle Joe in their digs.' [1]

Railways and Lancashire League cricket

An interesting means by which East Lancs rail services received a further boost during these years connected up with a heyday period in the popularity of Lancashire League cricket. The championship for a number of years was dominated by Nelson, who clinched the championship at will from 1928 and then virtually throughout the 30s. Their star player was renowned West Indian all-rounder Learie Constantine. His arrival in 1929 'sparked a run of highly dramatic batting and bowling feats...and also attracted ever-increasing numbers to pay their money to watch him perform.' [2]

Special trains were put on to accommodate the huge crowds travelling to see matches involving Nelson and Constantine, conveying thousands of passengers. It put a lot of pressure on the local rail stations of host cricket clubs. At Ramsbottom for example, arrangements were made with trains being stabled in the loops to the north of the level crossing.

Fred Hanson, a signalman at Rammy during these times, was later to recall: 'the local signalmen had their own grandstand view of the match. Ramsbottom South Box stood by the old *Square Works*, overlooking *Acre Bottom* cricket ground, and the men had put in their own 18-inch square window in the back of the box. On match day Sundays, when the box might be manned for an engineer's possession, the rostered signalman would have nothing to do but watch the game'.

Incidentally, Fred, having worked in both of the Ramsbottom crossing boxes, remembered the old L&YR model as 'poky, a queer little hole. Oil lamps inside before the 1930s, then gaslights, heavy levers facing the line, very limited clearance around the wheel which was parallel with the tracks, so you had to move front and back of it to get a view up and down the street'.[3]

The London, Midland and Scottish Railway

The LMS, which had taken over responsibility for East Lancashire railway lines from 1923 onwards, was a vast organisation. It was said to be the largest private enterprise in the world with 250,000 employees and about 7,000 miles of track. Even so, it took several years for the LMS to emerge as anything like a unified entity. Little was done to develop the former L&YR routes many of which in fairness ran parallel to ex-LNWR or ex-Midland routes now forming part of the same network.

LMS's greatest period of success coincided with the period William Stanier served from 1932 onwards as company locomotive engineer. The Duchess class *Pacifics* were a worthy rival to the magnificent *A4s* designed by Nigel Gresley running on London and North Eastern Railway (LNER) lines.

During the inter-war years, both companies struggled in terms of finding the money to invest in core services even if managing to capture positive headlines by competing for speed records. Although largely gaining the upper hand in this respect, through the feats of *Flying Scotsman* and *Mallard*, the LNER was hit much harder by the economic effects of the *Great Depression* of the 1930s. For, despite blistering records set on passenger runs, the LNER was essentially a freight railway with over 60% of its overall revenue based on goods traffic. During the *Depression*, there was a virtual collapse in the transport of industrial goods.

Growing road transport competition during the Inter-War Years

While the railway system in general endured protracted stagnation during the inter-war years, suffering from lack of extra investment, Government spending lent higher priority to road improvements. With the advent of mass production techniques in automobile manufacture, the number of private cars on the road doubled from 1 million at the start of the 1930s to 2 million by 1939. Although car ownership was still beyond the means of those on an average wage, bus transport had also come to present a major challenge to the railway system.

In 1930, responsibility for roads was vested in the County councils. The first inter-urban new road built in the UK was the 29.5 mile Liverpool-East Lancashire Road (colloquially known as the *East Lancs Road*) extending from Liverpool to Salford, 3 miles west of Manchester city centre. It was built between 1929 and 1934 at a cost of £8 million, superseding the existing hard-going A57 through Prescot, Warrington and Eccles. Providing much better access between the Port of Liverpool and the industrial areas of East Lancashire, journey times for road haulage would be reduced to under an hour.

As a result of the *Trunk Roads Act* of 1936, the Ministry of Transport took control of the core road network. Soon after, Lancashire County Council proposed a new scheme for a motorway and it was agreed to go ahead. This was, however, postponed due to the start of World War II in 1939. By comparison, the railway system was already plunged into a downward spiral with around 1,300 miles of passenger and freight railway line having already been closed between 1923 and 1939. Again it was very much a case of financial viability as to which lines survived and which went under.

World War Two

When war broke out in 1939, one of the first basic needs was to evacuate children away from city areas where they were at potential risk from bombing raids. The railway system played a crucial part in the safeguarding process. For example, many young children left the Newton Heath district of Manchester to be billeted in the Ramsbottom area. Margaret Hammersley later recalled the children arriving a few days after war had been declared on 3 September: 'When the evacuees came from Newton Heath, I was in the *St. John's Ambulance* and was at the station to meet the train. Many townspeople stood in the street weeping openly at the sight of the children with their gas masks. They were taken to *St. Paul's* and eventually found accommodation'. [4]

With the railway system also having a major role to play in the transfer of troops and armaments, ordinary passenger traffic was discouraged with slogans such as *'Is Your Journey Really Necessary?'* Whilst fares remained the same for people travelling to work-places, increases were imposed on fares for those on a leisure-outing. For example, 'basic return fares from Ramsbottom to Bury were raised from 7½d to 9½d.' [5]

Inevitably, at the war's end, the state took control again of the railway system in the same way it had done during World War One. The feeling had grown stronger to resist any temptation to put railways back into the hands of private companies.

Railway Nationalisation in 1948

The idea of bringing the railway system under state control had a long history going back to 1920. That was when Minister of Transport at the time Sir Eric Geddes had first put forward his proposal to nationalise railways. However, bearing in mind a post-war coalition government in power, there had not been sufficient support for it within Parliament as a whole. Instead, the *1921 Railway Act* had settled for a halfway house attempt at rationalisation by creating the *Big Four* – consisting of the Great Western Railway (GWR), London, Midland & Scottish Railway (LMS), London & North Eastern Railway (LNER) and Southern Railway (SR).

At the end of World War Two, the Labour Party had won the 1945 election with a landslide majority and taken the decision to nationalise Britain's run-down railway system. The 1947 *Transport Act* created the *British Transport Commission* to oversee the modernisation and integration not only of rail but also road, canal and air transport. From 1 January 1948, the railways were run by a body called the *Railway Executive*, answerable to the *BTC*.

From the outset, British Railways was faced with the enormous task of not only needing to repair about 20,000 miles of worn-out track and related infrastructure, but also of modernising and standardising its stock of over 20,000 steam engines, over one million goods wagons and over 55,000 passenger carriages.

British Railways was initially broken down into six geographical regions, almost replicating the make-up of the old *Big Four* railway companies. Although a degree of central control was built in, these regions possessed a fair amount of autonomy – a situation that did not lend itself to an integrated rail system or standardisation of resources from the outset.

Knowsley Street station – Footbridge Accident in 1952

The early post-war years witnessed two serious misfortunes at each of the two Bury stations. The first occurred at Bolton Street on 14 May 1947 when a fire destroyed buildings at ground street level. It was not until 1952 that the station's front area, built with brick and concrete, was re-opened. Unhappily, in this same year, tragedy occurred at Knowsley Street station. On Saturday 19 January, *Bury F.C.* played host to *Blackburn Rovers* at *Gigg Lane.* After the final whistle blew, nearly 3,000 away supporters headed home via Knowsley Street where the trains were to take them back to Blackburn.

However, a platform footbridge collapsed under the weight of the number of people attempting to cross it, collapsing from a height of 15 feet down to rail level. The station master, standing on the Down platform, had belatedly heard the bridge timbers creaking, and seen the bridge collapse and hit the ground below with resounding impact. One person was killed and 173 injured, with 136 taken to *Bury Hospital.*

It was thought that the footbridge had been put up seventy or so years earlier. In the course of the inquest that followed, no detailed drawings were found to ascertain the exact date. A new footbridge was put up in 1953 in exactly the same position, although this time made of steel with a concrete deck. This bridge later came to be dismantled and removed when Knowsley Street was demolished in 1971.

BR *Modernisation Plan* of 1955

Across the national railway system as a whole, there was a call for '*Modernisation*'. The plan, devised in 1955, would spell the end of steam locomotive haulage and the introduction of diesel-electric locomotives, a type of engine which had been patented by the

German engineer Rudolf Diesel in 1892. This change-over appeared heavily influenced by experience learnt from North America. Over recent years, railroads in the United States had largely done away with steam in favour of diesel locomotives. What gave added incentive to the transition was the pressure facing BR of mounting competition from other modes of transport together with the need to increase rail safety and efficiency.

Diesel traction was perceived to have a number of advantages. Firstly, it could operate for long periods with no lost maintenance time. Secondly, it used less fuel energy than a steam locomotive, because its thermal efficiency was about four times greater. Thirdly, it could accelerate a train more rapidly and operate at higher sustained speeds with less damage to the track. The alternative had been under consideration for some time previously without being acted upon. Following years of inaction on the part of the *Big Four* railway companies, the start of World War II had delayed any widespread dieselisation of passenger service. It was not to be until the mid-1950s that British Railways embarked upon a systematic £2,000,000 programme targeted at the development of lightweight diesel trains – *DMUs* (diesel multiple units).

The Bury to Bacup line in East Lancashire was selected to be one of the first in the country to receive the new *DMUs*. The first trial took place in 1954 using a *Derby* lightweight with further testing taking place during 1955. The plan was for these units to replace the steam-hauled Bacup/Bury/ Manchester service via Heywood and Moston and also the Bury to Bacup services from 6 February 1956 onwards. Bury Shed took delivery of seven twin car sets built by Metro Cammell. Numbered *79076 – 82* (motor coach) and *79626 – 32* (driving trailer), precursors of the large *101* fleet which followed. In August 1955, the first lightweight diesel car, produced by Metro Cammell, had emerged from Washwood Heath works at Saltley in Birmingham.

The sets allocated to Bury worked regular trips to Manchester Victoria during December 1955 and January 1956. From Bury to Bacup, the weekday services doubled to half-hourly frequency with 35 trains on weekdays and 47 on Saturdays with the journey time reduced from 37 to 34 minutes. In the first six days of operation, 23,000 passengers travelled, compared with 8,000 in the same period by steam in the previous year. Later figures released in July 1956 showed 156,317 passengers had travelled on the Bury-Bacup line since the diesel service had started on 6 February 1956, an increase in take-up of 35%, appearing to demonstrate the capacity of the diesel service to revive the fortunes of local rail routes. In the meantime, BR had continued to commit to its programme of *DMU* building to replace the ageing steam fleet.

Diesel services were extended from 6 March 1961 following the arrival of 25 *Cravens* built twin sets. They took over services between Manchester Victoria and Colne, via Clifton Junction, Bury and Accrington, between Preston and Colne and between Manchester Victoria and Blackburn via Bolton. Each of these routes was put on an hourly interval basis giving two trains per hour for most of the day between Accrington and Colne. At the same time, the Manchester to Colne train connected at Accrington with the Colne to Preston affording a second opportunity each hour to reach Blackburn from Manchester in a time which was no longer than that taken by the direct service via Bolton.

Rescue of a number of steam engines

While steam engines might not have lost any of their appeal to many, Rail bosses seemed convinced that their days were over. Many such once-grand locomotives were written off as rust-buckets. However, some wealthier members of '*Generation Steam*' were not about to see them consigned to oblivion. For example, in 1959, Captain Bill Smith, an ex-naval officer, invested in the preservation of a tank engine: *Class J52 68846*. It had famously served as a pilot engine at King's Cross '*Top Shed*', shifting the Gresley *Pacifics* and other star attractions around when they were not in steam. According to an article on the *NRM* website about *68846*, 'This was the first mainline locomotive to be bought by an individual for preservation, and it made many people sit up and take notice – including Alan Pegler, who later bought '*Flying Scotsman*'.

Meanwhile, certain steam engines became attractions in new, unfamiliar settings. For example, the *LMS Coronation class 46229 Duchess of Hamilton,* built in 1938 at Crewe, was saved from the scrapyard, along with classmate *46233 Duchess of Sutherland*, as a result of Sir Billy Butlin's efforts to install these locomotives as children's playground exhibits at his Minehead holiday camp in 1964.

By way of postscript, in 1976, the *Friends of the National Railway Museum* accepted the *Duchess of Hamilton* on a twenty-year loan deal, and immediately began to restore and preserve it. After purchasing the locomotive from *Butlin's* in 1987, an extensive overhaul saw it running again in 1989 until withdrawn from main line duty in 1996 when its seven-year boiler ticket expired. Two years later, the ELR was destined to be closely involved with the final 'bowing out' of the famous *46229*.

Flying Scotsman

Alan Pegler was for ever to be associated with this most famous of steam engines, destined in later years to grace the lines of the re-opened East Lancashire Railway, amongst many others. Born in 1920, Pegler had hero-worshipped the locomotive since the age of four after being lifted onto its footplate when it was displayed at Wembley in 1924 at the *British Empire Exhibition*. The *4-6-2 Pacific* steam locomotive had been built in 1923 for the London and North Eastern Railway (LNER) as a Class *A1* locomotive built to the design of famous rail engineer Nigel Gresley. It was in February 1924 that, as well as being assigned a new number - *4472* - the locomotive acquired its name after *The Flying Scotsman* express service which operated from 1862 onwards between London King's Cross and Edinburgh Waverley. [6]

In 1928, the LNER decided to make *The Flying Scotsman* a non-stop service for the first time. Soon after, the service's flagship locomotive of the same name had gone on to achieve two significant world records: the longest non-stop run by a steam engine – 393 miles between London and Edinburgh – in 1928. Then, on 30 November 1934, *Flying Scotsman* became the first steam locomotive to reach an officially authenticated speed of 100 mph (161 km/h).

Following the nationalisation of Britain's railways in 1948, almost all of LNER's engine numbers were changed, with *Flying Scotsman* becoming *60103.* On 4 June 1950, now under BR ownership, the locomotive was allocated to a new base at Leicester Central on the Great Central Railway. It returned to the East Coast Main Line in 1953, initially based in Grantham before returning to King's Cross in April 1954, where it remained until the early 60s. When British Railways had announced in 1962 its intention to scrap *Flying Scotsman*, a group called *'Save Our Scotsman'* formed but was unable to raise the £3,000 scrap value of the locomotive that would prevent its demise..

Alan Pegler: Steam Railway Enthusiast Extraordinary

With the *Scotsman* seemingly doomed to extinction, it was Pegler who rescued the engine from the breaker's yard, raising the money required from his share of the proceeds accruing to him from the recent sale of the family firm, *Pegler's Valves.*

It is an understatement to say that Pegler was a rail enthusiast. Previously, he had committed himself to preserving the Ffestiniog narrow gauge mountain railway in North Wales that ran for 13 miles (21k) from the slate quarries at Blaenau Ffestiniog to the seaport town of Portmadog. It certainly helped that he had private financial backing. Lent £3,000 by his father, he had obtained control and was appointed the company's chairman.

When asked what he found fascinating about *Flying Scotsman*, Pegler's simple reply had been: 'It was the colour really.' What had left an indelible impression that time at Wembley was the big, highly polished, bright green engine, compared with the relatively drab, dark Brunswick green '*Great Western Castle*' that stood next to it.

Now, after taking it upon himself to save *Flying Scotsman*, Pegler next had to pay out ever larger sums of money to have the locomotive restored at the Doncaster Works to restore it to full working order, not to mention making it look resplendent again in its original LNER green livery. Pegler managed to persuade British Railways management to enter into a contract to let him run *Flying Scotsman* excursions on line, at that time the *Scotsman* being the only steam locomotive still running on mainline British Railways.

Transport Act of 1962 and the 'Beeching Cuts'

Although the entrepreneurial initiatives of the likes of Pegler acted as a partial brake on the scrapping of steam engines, the existing rail system as a whole was now subjected to a far more serious threat than ever encountered before.

Introduced by a Conservative government, the 1962 *Transport Act*, doing away with the *British Transport Commission*, appeared to grant British Railways complete autonomy as to how it acted as an independent public corporation. With effect from 1 January 1963, the new *British Railways Board*, led by former *BTC* Chairman Dr. Richard Beeching, was charged with drawing up action plans to address the problem of ever-increasing national railway deficits. Beeching's services did not come cheaply though. His substantive post at the time was as a director of *ICI* (*Imperial Chemical Industries*) from which company he was granted a sabbatical in order to come up with a plan to address issues relating to the national rail network.

'Part of the deal was that Beeching's *ICI* salary would be matched. This brought him £24,000 a year - £10,000 more than the Prime Minister... However, for this he was expected to deliver a solution to the problem of making the railways pay.' [7]

§

This was not though the first time that actions had been taken to address the problem. About 3,000 miles of rail line, seen as uneconomic to run, had been closed following nationalisation in 1948. The same was true with regard to railway stations. For example, in East Lancashire, Haslingden station had been closed to passengers in 1960, less than a year before the diesel trains were introduced. Haslingden's isolated location on the edge of town had always been a disadvantage access-wise as far as passenger traffic was concerned.

The declared reason for closing Haslingden had been cited as addressing unnecessary extra costs. BR's contention was that its station staff were occupied for no more than 15% of their time at work and most of what they did was just "flunkeyism" - e.g. helping people on and off trains. [8]

Meanwhile Baxenden station, also positioned an awkward distance from centre of town, had been closed for passenger services even earlier in 1951 and for freight traffic in 1961. Post-war enhancement of bus transport services was also a contributory factor to station closures in both instances.

The Bury to Holcombe Brook branch line was another example of cutbacks pre-Beeching. In 1938, there had been 29 return trips on weekdays. This service had continued into BR days but on 25 March 1951 the electric trains were replaced by steam push-pulls, pending anticipated renewal of the electrical equipment. However, the overhaul never took place and the passenger service had been completely withdrawn on 4 May 1952. Goods traffic continued to be handled until 1960 when the branch was cut back from Bury to Tottington. This truncated stretch of the branch line survived only until August 1963, never thereafter to be restored to use as a railway. By way of postscript, the extinct railway line linking Bury town centre and Greenmount was destined to become better known in more recent times as the '*Kirklees Trail*', providing pathway access through the *Kirklees Valley Local Nature Reserve* for the benefit of walkers and cyclists.

Government's new agenda

Despite the closure of about 3,000 miles of line since nationalisation in 1948, there was a firm belief at governmental level that vast amounts of public money were still being squandered in subsidising an antiquated and overmanned railway system.

In the event, Beeching wasted little time in producing the first of his two reports, '*The Reshaping of British Railways*' (1963), identifying 2,263 new stations and 5,000 miles of railway line ear-marked for closure, amounting to 55% of stations, 30% of route miles, with 67,700 jobs to be shed. At the same time, locomotive numbers were to be reduced by 9,000 with 16,000 carriages and 450,000 freight wagons scrapped. [9]

Although Beecham came up with his reports, it was suspected he was merely the mouthpiece of Ernest Marples, Minister of Transport from 1959 to 1964. Marples had little time for rail transport, cutting a dash behind the wheel of fast cars and having a vested interest in supporting the bids of commercial companies to construct roads, despite being at taxpayers' expense.

The word 'scientific' was a favoured one in Marples' vocabulary. It was believed he had taken on Dr. Beeching as his protégé for the reason that the latter's PhD was in Physics. The fact that he had no existing experience of railways certainly didn't go against Beeching, if anything the opposite. Despite his portly, rather old-school appearance, he was touted as offering an 'outside the box' approach.

Effects of the Beeching Report on East Lancashire

In specific relation to East Lancashire , the *Beeching Report* projection could hardly have been more damning. It recommended closure of all the routes between Manchester, Bury, Bacup and Accrington, including the electric service. The Rochdale to Bolton service was listed amongst those 'to be modified'. It was soon confirmed that this actually meant 'withdrawn'.

By way of overall remit, something of a procedural safety-net clause was built in to the terms of the *Beeching Report*, allowing rail travellers the right to respond to its findings. Bodies were set up to handle public reaction, called *Transport Users' Consultative Committees* (*TUCCs*). The first line in East Lancashire to be subject to this procedure was the electric service from Manchester to Bury. When a formal closure notice was issued in January 1964, it raised a public outcry with the *TUCC* in question being bombarded by more than a thousand written objections. With the *TUCC* reporting back that unnecessary hardship would ensue, closure of the line was eventually set to be refused in January 1965.

Not much else though seemed to stand in the way of the sweeping programme of closures put forward. For example, the hourly Manchester to Colne service was curtailed in September 1964 to run only between Bury and Accrington. Only a sparse service remained between Clifton Junction and Bury. At the same time, the Rochdale to Bolton line lost its Sunday trains.

Shortly afterwards, closure notices were published concerning routes from Clifton Junction through Bury to Bacup and Accrington, also from Castleton to Bolton via Bury Knowsley Street. It was perhaps surprising that the Bury-Bacup line did not survive the Beeching cuts. However, the case for closure had been argued on quoted evidence of over-manned stations, loss-making goods facilities and reduced passenger numbers.

Despite such strongly-argued assertions, certain local areas still put up particularly strong opposition to the so-called findings. For example, Summerseat residents protested that their village lay in danger of being cut off if the Bury to Bacup line was closed and that any proposed replacement bus service didn't take account of the fact that road access in and out of Summerseat was very difficult due to steep gradients.

Objections took a wide range of forms. For example, *Rawtenstall Cricket Club* claimed 'the closure would have a detrimental effect on the number of spectators attending to watch matches...The *Workers Educational Association* said the closure would affect the quality of the classes held in Rossendale, as many of the tutors travelled from Manchester and the loss of the trains would make their journeys more complicated. [10]

There was no quick response from the government to all the various objections raised. With a General Election in prospect, the situation was not helped by a prevailing climate of uncertainty as to which political party might ultimately end up having to make the vital decisions.

A Change of Government in 1964

Following 13 years of Conservative government, the General Election of October 1964 had returned a Labour government under Prime Minister Harold Wilson. During the election campaign, Labour had pledged to halt rail closures if elected but then appeared to backtrack after winning the nation's vote. Meanwhile, the second of Beeching's reports, *'The Development of the Major Railway Trunk Routes' (1965),* had seemed more conciliatory in tone, setting out ways in which the surviving railway network might be modernised and streamlined. Of the 7,500 remaining miles of main line trunk railway, 3,000 were 'chosen for further development'.

Beeching's aim appeared to be to whittle the national railway system down to a core of inter-city lines in the optimistic belief that people would drive to the stations on these lines – the 'rail-heads' – to board the trains. The 'streamlining' was such that for example, all train traffic to Wales would be funnelled through Swansea; large parts of East Anglia would have no railways; the East Coast Main Line would be closed north of Newcastle. The report ended up being rejected as far too drastic by the Labour Transport Secretary, Tom Fraser. Meanwhile, Beeching had been released from his Government-attached post and was back in his substantive role with *ICI*.

In December 1965, Blackburn MP Barbara Castle became Labour Transport Secretary. Her stance appeared to be more understanding of the broader social issues, sounding prepared to provide 'subsidies' to keep lines open that were 'socially necessary'. The decisions which were finally announced in September 1966 seemed a 'mixed economy' across the board. In specific relation to East Lancashire, the sections of line from Clifton Junction to Bury, from Stubbins Junction to Accrington and from Rawtenstall to Bacup were set to close but the stretch from Bury Bolton Street to Rawtenstall was to continue, offering relief to the residents of Summerseat. Withdrawal of the Rochdale to Bolton service was also refused with the ministerial response hinting that a better long-term solution might be found in the introduction of an express bus service.

Despite certain decisions being made, there were still though a large number of questions remaining unanswered.

Notes

1. Margaret Ferguson, *A Rammy Childhood 1924-34* in *Ramsbottom Reminiscences Volumes 1 & 2, pub.* 2022 by Ramsbottom Heritage Society (ed. Andrew Todd) pp. 116-7
2. Nigel Jepson, *175 Not Out – The Story of Ramsbottom Cricket Club*, pub. in 2022 by YouCaxton, p.34

3. Andrew Todd article in *Memories of Ramsbottom Signal Box and Crossings*: RHS Magazine No. 19, Spring 2000, p.10.
4. Ramsbottom Heritage Society Commemorative '*War News*' Issue no. 1: *Preparing for War,* pub. *2010, p.5*
5. RHS '*War News*' Issue no. 4: *1942* p.15
6. *The Flying Scotsman*, 1925, pub. LNER, p.4
7. Greg Morse, *British Railways in the 1950s and '60s*, pub 2012 by Shire Library, p.31
8. *Modern Railways* – April 1963
9. *The Reshaping of British Railways*, pub. British Rail, 1963 p. 50
10. Andy Coward, *East Lancashire Railway,* pub. Mortons Media Group Ltd, 2018 pp. 14-15

Dr Beeching presents his damning report 1963

A winter's day at Clough Fold station mid 1960s

Helmshore station 1966

Police presence at Summerseat Station - Jan 1967

Alan Pegler and daughter Penny

Ramsbottom 1972 last train

Breaking through the banner at Bury Bolton Street on 25 July 1987

Trevor Jones

New Ramsbottom Station - officially opened 19 June 1989

Reopening of Rawtenstall station 1991

Irwell Vale station

Gothenburg

Chapter Seven – '*Beeching Cuts*' take effect

Events in Helmshore: 1966

The announcement of the closure of the Ramsbottom to Accrington line certainly raised the hackles of a tight-knit group of people in Helmshore upset at the prospect of no longer being able to commute to Manchester by train.

Letters sent to the Prime Minister and to the Secretary of State for Transport eventually produced a response to the effect that Mrs. Castle was not prepared to interfere with the decision already announced. As something of a last throw of the dice, a public meeting had been arranged to take place in Helmshore on 25 November 1966, just one week before the scheduled closure of the line.

With the intention of forming a Helmshore and District Railway Preservation Society (H&DRPS), Walter Baker was chosen to address the meeting. He had experience of dealing with such situations as a prominent member of West Yorkshire's Keighley and Worth Valley Railway Preservation Society (KWVRPS), formed after that railway had been ear-marked for closure in 1962. KWVRPS had been successful in buying back the line from BR, who allowed the Society to pay the sum in instalments. It was to re-open as a heritage railway on 29 June 1968.

Baker was persuasive in putting his case forward. By the end of the meeting, an eight-member *Helmshore Society Council* had been formed, including three representatives of the local authority, Haslingden Corporation. The aim was to maintain the life of the passenger commuter section of line from Stubbins to Accrington, including Helmshore station.

However, on Saturday 3 December 1966, final train runs took place on three condemned sections of line, including that from

Stubbins to Accrington. At Helmshore, the sole station on the line to have survived to this point, hundreds of local people and enthusiasts turned out on the day to mark the occasion. The train bore the same coat of arms as the original East Lancashire Railway Company had done when the line had been opened back in 1848.

Ernest Dewhurst reported in *The Guardian*: 'For many, the farewell meant a trip to Bury and back on the last diesel...Fog detonators were exploded, but everything revolved around the local brass band, which had been founded not long after the line had first been opened'. [1]

Members of *Helmshore Local History Society*, such as Chris Aspin, a founding member, were active in proceedings. Living in Helmshore, Chris' work as a journalist involved travelling by train to Manchester where he was employed with the *Manchester Evening News*, writing chiefly on business, finance and music, whilst also acting as local correspondent for *The Times, The Guardian* and *The Daily Telegraph*.

Chris contacted the *British Museum* to obtain a copy of the score of the '*Excursion Train Gallop*', a work written in 1844 which had been played at the time of the opening of the railway line in 1848. Receiving a copy back, he had contacted Herbert Farnworth, aged 89 of Loveclough, to ask him to arrange the score in advance of the 'event' set to take place on Saturday 3 December at Helmshore station.

Although the score had only come into the hands of the *Helmshore Prize Band* on the Saturday morning itself, the band made best use of the short time available. As Ernest Dewhurst continued in his report: 'Direct from rehearsals in a former teetotallers' club, the *Sunny Bank Social Club*, the band then found itself a pool of gaslight on the station platform and plunged into the '*Excursion Train Gallop*' and other pieces including '*Eldorado*' and '*Federation*'.

Chris Aspin was also inspired to pen a poem, which appeared in the following Monday's edition of *the Guardian* as follows:

'In Memoriam' - The Stubbins-Accrington Line

Opened August 17, 1848 Closed December 3, 1966
Old line farewell. Now useless you must lie
In mute rebuke of those who let you die.

A hundred years ago we watched you come
Arching the cliffs of Ravenshore and Lumb,
Slicing the hills and leaping every stream
To lay the path of progress and of steam.
(How swift your triumph and how great the power
Of trains that 'flew' at 30 miles an hour).
Gone is that Age of Progress, gone the day
When planners worked to make the railway pay.
Mocked and abused you were; but yet you showed
One way to miss the chaos of the road.
The signal falls, the last train rounds the bend,
The gates are closed, your life is at an end. [2]

§

Around 400 passengers boarded at Helmshore for the last train journey. On the station platform, the band also played '*Auld Lang Syne*', accompanied by an emotional vocal outpouring from those crowding round on the station platform. Then, with a last blow on the whistle, the train moved off to Accrington.

The H&DRPS seemed at first to make good progress. In May 1967, it formally took on the lease of Helmshore station on an initial three-month basis. Hoping to proceed in the same manner as the Keighley and Worth Valley RPS, the Society aimed to purchase the line from BR in annual instalments. However, the 'deal' that the KWVRPS had struck was sadly one that BR was unwilling to replicate. The only option given the H&DRPS was to make an up-front one-off payment. This was way beyond its means to deliver.

A mood of frustration took over. Only negative replies had been received from the various bodies approached for assistance. Attendance at the monthly Council meetings began to wane, significantly that of local authority representatives. By April 1968, rumours were rife that Haslingden Corporation was seeking to purchase part of the track bed for some kind of non-railway use. A general meeting was called to disband the Society. Thirty people attended and the resolution to wind up was passed. At this point, Walter Baker, obdurate as ever, stood up and asked whether there was anyone present interested in preserving part of the line for 'enthusiasts services' – in effect changing tack to becoming a heritage line.

A few hands were raised and these people were asked to stay behind for further discussion. As a result of the short meeting that took place after, the East Lancashire Railway Preservation Society (ELRPS) came into being with Walter Baker as Chairman, Hilda Rogals Vice Chairman and Peter Lord (with a membership number of 007 that he retains to the present day) serving as Treasurer. The ELRPS held its first Council Meeting on Tuesday 21 May 1968 and on 28 May had a meeting with British Railways. There was still hope!

Summerseat takes action: 1967

When the Bury-Bacup line was threatened with closure, there had been strong protests from the villagers of Summerseat. A *Rail Action Committee* was formed and letters publicising concerns were fired off near and far. One was even sent to the United Nations.

The villagers were understandably jubilant when the announcement was made by Minister of Transport, Barbara Castle, in September 1966 that the section of line between Bury and Rawtenstall had been reprieved although not as far as Bacup. So it was that on Saturday, 3 December 1966, the 11.45 pm train from Rawtenstall – packed with enthusiasts and local people – was the last to Bacup.

A sting in the tail though to the Bury-Rawtenstall 'reprieve' was that the service now operated less frequently. Piqued by this, campaigners decided to take fresh action and mount a major protest event in the new year. On a cold Saturday in January 1967, a well-organised crowd of about 150 local residents turned up at Summerseat station. *The Burnley Evening Star*, in its edition of 16 January, chronicled happenings on the day in its step-by-step account:

'1.55 pm – Villagers, police and a BBC film team crowd the platform...demonstrators carry posters coloured shocking pink: '*Barbara Castle must go*' and '*Stop the train drain*'...

2.16 pm – The Rawtenstall-Bury train is now due. A woman walks on to the line...Two transport policewomen walk towards her...A man on the line is told by police: 'You are being reported for the offence of trespassing on the railway.'

2.25 pm – The train rolls into Summerseat to mixed cheers and jeers.

2.29 pm – It looks as if the train has cleared the demonstrators. But suddenly, at the last moment, the brakes go on as a man walks out from hiding to sit down on the rails a few feet from the train and forces a four minute halt to British Rail's new train schedule. The smell of success is in the air as children sing: "Where have all the trains gone?" '[3]

However, BR dug its heels in further. From March 1968 onwards, BR cost-saving exercises meant stations on the line were left unstaffed and open to vandalism. A few months later, BR began single-line operations on the route, with the disused second line lifted for scrap.

At a public inquiry held on 29 October 1970, Bury Council announced it was spending £35,000 on road improvements, enabling bus services to operate more effectively. This couldn't help but take the wind out of the sails of the Summerseat villagers' argument that, without the continued existence of the rail connection, the community would be exposed to isolation.

The Final Reckoning: 1972

One of Barbara Castle's last initiatives as Transport Minister had been the *Transport Act* of 1968. As well as the provision of subsidies for rail services, the Act had set up *Passenger Transport Executives* (*PTEs*) aimed at achieving a stronger degree of co-ordination at local level. Five such *PTEs* were put in place. The *PTE* charged with co-ordinating developments in East Lancashire was *SELNEC* (South East Lancashire & North East Cheshire). From 1 November 1969 onwards, this new body had responsibility for deciding the fate of existing rail lines within its area.

The network around Bury found itself coming under ever-increasing scrutiny. At this point, it still had passenger trains radiating out in four directions: to Manchester, Rawtenstall, Rochdale and Bolton. However, the future looked bleak for three of those four services. Events unfolded in stages. In January 1969, the Bury-Rawtenstall line had been granted the first of two one-year reprieves. The second was given twelve months later. However, the Minister had stipulated that he 'would require more cogent evidence of need' before extending it beyond 1971.

An important public hearing took place in Bury on 29 October 1970. It was the same meeting, previously referred to, at which Bury Council announced intent to invest £35,000 in road improvements in the Summerseat district. In advance of this public hearing, seven local authorities and 66 individuals had submitted written objections to the newly-proposed closure of the Bury to Rawtenstall line. To no avail however. The decision was made in early 1972 by the Minister of Transport to reverse the reprieve that had come about six years earlier. It was hoped that *SELNEC* would intervene but this did not happen.

Meanwhile another line scheduled for closure in June 1972 was the Oldham to Rochdale. In this instance, *SELNEC* did come in with a last-minute rescue package. Although originally meant only to last six months, in the event the line was destined to survive into the next century. The reason given for the stay of execution on the Oldham to Rochdale was to allow time to consider whether the line had a place in future development plans, mainly as a feeder contribution to the proposed Manchester Piccadilly/Victoria ('*Picc-Vic*') line. Many thought the Bury-Rawtenstall line might have served the purpose better but *SELNEC* declared in favour of the Oldham-Rochdale connection.

With the die now cast for the Bury-Rawtenstall passenger service, the process of dismantling its infrastructure went on apace. The year 1971 was to witness stations all along the track being demolished as a prelude to the closing of the line as a whole. For example, Ramsbottom station was closed down in early January 1972: 'The ticket office at Ramsbottom railway station is being taken down piece by piece this weekend. Within days it is likely there will be nothing left of the once busy station, opened in 1846. All that will stand on the platform is a temporary wooden shelter put up for passengers...The office is being taken down by hand because it is made of the best dressed stone...For many people, the station was not just a building...it was part of the character of the town.' [4]

Summerseat, Stubbins, Ewood Bridge and Rawtenstall stations suffered the same fate. Only Bury Bolton Street station kept open. This was on account of the electric service which operated to Manchester. However, Bolton Street was by this point not a patch on its former self. The old ELR headquarter building for example had by the early 70s fallen into disuse, now nothing more than a convenient storage facility for BR. The building which had been a style icon in its heyday was eventually deemed unsafe and was knocked down in 1974.

In January 1972, the closure of the Bury-Rawtenstall passenger service had been confirmed by the Minister of Transport. Thereafter, BR gave four months' notice of its intention to abandon the Bury-Rawtenstall line, announcing that the final trains would run on Saturday 3 June 1972. Having suffered declining numbers over previous years, it was ironic that the final train services on 3 June needed to be strengthened to a four-car unit to accommodate the hundreds of people who turned out to witness the parting of the last passenger train between Rawtenstall and Bury – the 9.05 pm.

There was added poignancy to the occasion given that passenger facilities by this time had been reduced to small wooden bus stop-style waiting shelters. The travellers on the last passenger train participated in a sad event marking the end of a 126-year long record of continuous passenger service. At the time, any hope of travelling again by train on this line seemed impossible. Clutching at straws, the line did continue to be used for freight purposes, conveying coal to Rawtenstall..

Mood amongst local rail enthusiasts

To many rail enthusiasts who had grown up from childhood with a love of steam engines, the cuts of the 1960s proved a hard reality check. For example, Richard Law, now in his mid-70s, recalls the prevalent mood of the times. He had become involved in the local situation in 1969, having arrived at Helmshore after his father had moved from his previous job in Darwen to become General Manager of the

Rossendale Joint Transport Committee, preceding the establishment of the *Rossendale Borough Council* in 1974. At the time, Richard was employed by BR in a civil engineering post which, although based in Preston, involved him travelling a lot around the country.

Like many others with a passion for railways, Richard felt a need to ensure that the values and traditions of the past should be maintained in a positive way. Following this instinct, he had become a member of the East Lancashire Railway Preservation Society recently formed in Helmshore.

The East Lancashire Railway Preservation Society: 1968 to 1972

Since it had come into being in 1968, the ELRPS had kept on fighting the closure of the Stubbins-Accrington line. By the end of 1968, the Society had a membership of 120 and raised £150. Although hardly a staggering sum of money, it was useful for the purpose of entering into further negotiations with BR for the return of the line back into local hands. However, the scale of the challenge facing the new group was put into stark perspective at a meeting with BR in January 1969 when the price for taking over the line was set at £40,000 for the track and £6,000 for the land.

Unfortunately, by this time, support from Haslingden Corporation had evaporated with many of its representatives making no bones about their opposition to the Society's plans. For example, Councillor Ervin Russell stated: 'In my opinion, they are crackpots and they just want to play at being railwaymen. They are playing like a lot of children and this is a lot of nonsense. They are interfering with progress in the town...they are a pack of loonies and a blithering nuisance.'

The ELRPS was not daunted though in the face of such scathing remarks. For example, whilst discussions continued, volunteers had been working hard in tidying up Helmshore station, which was still being rented from British Rail pending the future of the line being decided upon. Meanwhile in 1970, a couple of well-attended open days at the station had taken place, allowing visitors to learn more about the project.

Having the use of the station was one thing but buying the line another. For one thing, British Rail would not deal with an unincorporated society. It was necessary therefore for a *Limited Liability Company* to be formed. Hence the East Lancashire Light Railway Company Limited came into existence on 6 January 1970 in order to maintain the option of negotiating. However, in Spring 1971, BR had made a further ultimatum concerning the large sum of money they were requiring the Society to pay for the line, together with the station premises at Helmshore. Richard Law recalled that the message BR sent out at this point was: 'Buy it or move out!' It dawned on the Society at this point that its goals were unachievable and that it needed to re-evaluate its plans.

As reported in *The Guardian*: 'Mr Chris Bates, Secretary, issued a statement as spokesperson for the ELRPS: "We have tried to persuade BR to reduce the price further but without success. Now we are looking round for new headquarters." [5]

At the Society's Annual Meeting in June 1971, there were quite a few members who favoured disbanding but others seemed willing to continue. Even the most die-hard of optimists were left having to concede though that the Helmshore based side of the project had failed and that they now needed to look for an alternative site. The urgency to do so was reinforced by an ultimatum given by BR to vacate Helmshore by 21 June. A number of different sites came under scrutiny. Harry Brierley, a member of the Society and employee of BR, suggested the former ELR Castlecroft goods warehouse at Bury Bolton Street station as a future base for the Society. Harry lived in Ramsbottom and travelled daily by train to Manchester, passing the Castlecroft site which was being used by contractors building *Peel Way*, part of the Bury bypass road system.

The yard surrounding the warehouse had been drastically reduced in size as a result of the road construction, but, with the project completed, the road contractors had left. There was still enough of the yard surviving though to allow events to take place that would attract public interest. Castlecroft was also handily placed, sitting adjacent to the Bury to Rawtenstall line. An added bonus came with Bury Council letting the ELRPS have the site on a peppercorn rent.

The lease obtained from Bury County Borough Council was initially on a one-year basis. Meanwhile, members recognised there was no time to be lost in clearing up the mess left behind by the contractors. During the rest of that first year, the ELRPS embarked on the process of transferring merchandise from Helmshore to its new home in Bury with keys to Helmshore station having been returned to BR.

In order to fill space at Castlecroft, the Society first approached the *Crossley Omnibus Society* and owners of other preserved road vehicles, offering them space in the newly-created '*Museum*'. In addition, several other attractions had been added for the purpose, including locomotives, rolling stock, various railway memorabilia, buses, lorries and a working steamroller, '*Hilda*', named after the wife of its original owner, the founder of *R & T Howarth*, Civil Engineers of Rochdale. In due course, the site was officially declared open by the Mayor of Bury, Councillor David Owen Davies on Saturday 26 August 1972. To further attract visitors, a loco was steamed on the last Sunday of each month giving footplate rides in the yard in return for a donation.

The move from Helmshore to Castlecroft was a brave step for the Society to have undertaken in the first place, let alone taking on the challenge of re-opening the Bury-Rawtenstall line. There were many though who thought it was only setting itself unachievable targets again.

Helmshore Postscript

This chapter started with describing events in Helmshore that took place in 1966. The author wanted though to find out what happened to the station and the line in the years since the late 1960s.

In December 2022, in the company of Richard Law, I was grateful to him for taking me round Helmshore in his Land Rover, explaining that the rail track had been lifted in 1971 with a significant part of the trackbed between Haslingden and Rising Bridge lost during the construction of the Haslingden road by-pass.

At certain points, Richard parked up and showed me the few remaining pieces of evidence of Helmshore's railway past. For example, on Helmshore Road, clambering out of the Land Rover and, despite the ground being extremely icy underfoot, we inched forward to view an original level crossing gate-post with a brass plaque attached reading: '*Helmshore Railway Opened 17th August 1848, Closed 3rd December 1966*'.

Helmshore station had remained derelict, although virtually still intact, until the early 1980s when the main station buildings and platforms were demolished. The site itself is now occupied by cottages which have been built over the former trackbed and platforms. The former goods yard is now the site of a small industrial estate.

Two particular residences in the vicinity however provide interesting evidence of the one-time railway connection. First is the '*Station Master's House*', now privately owned, which is situated on the Bury side of the former level crossing. Secondly, standing adjacent to the *Station Master's House*, is another building lying on the site of what was once the old signal box bearing an inscription saying it was bought and re-designed by Mr Allan Dunn. Having obtained planning permission to convert the building, he demolished it and re-built it to the same design as the original. The letters '*LMS*' are carved on the wall by way of testimony to past times. Other than these vestiges of the past, Helmshore's railway history appeared to have almost completely vanished with the passage of time.

Not quite so in relation to the Stubbins-Helmshore line though. Although the track was taken up and never re-laid, it is still possible to walk or cycle the original route. In so doing, one can for example cross the famous Lumb Viaduct, eulogised in Chris Aspin's poem of 1966. Grade II listed in 1984, restoration work was carried out in 2015 to bring the viaduct into use as part of the *National Cycle Network*. From the valley below, one is left gasping in admiration at the 65-high foot structure comprising nine segmental arches, each 40 feet in span, engineered by the original ELR's John Shae Perring and Sturges Meek back in 1848.

Notes

1. *Guardian*, 5 December 1966
2. As for Item above
3. *Burnley Evening Star*, 16 January 1967

4. *Bury Times*, 9 January 1971
5. *Guardian*, 6 May 1971

Chapter Eight – *The Phoenix* rises

Negotiating with BR over the Bury-Rawtenstall Rail Track-Bed

In 1973, a promising opportunity opened up with the ELRPS obtaining from BR over a 'Quarter Mile' of track-bed alongside the Rawtenstall line. Once the track had been laid and connected to the Castlecroft Museum yard, it became possible to offer longer footplate rides to rail enthusiasts. At one stage, the Society believed agreement had been reached, at least in principle, with local BR management to allow it to operate more broadly on the line. However, in August 1973, BR announced that its policy forbade any preservation society to 'share' tracks. This was in the context of the continued use of the line to transport coal to the depot at Rawtenstall.

Building on the Museum site

In May 1975, a '*Schools Week*' took place with pupils able to see a locomotive in steam. Eleven hundred children visited the site with many taking a short ride on the footplate of the loco. This was the first of many such schools weeks. Work continued on the Castlecroft site. *The Refreshment Room*, the small exhibits display and the *Museum Shop* were all enlarged to cater for an increasing number of visitors. At this stage though, the main source of income came through house-to-house newspaper collections on Tuesday evenings which were bundled up for delivery to a paper mill. Footplate rides came to be banned after 1976 following an accident elsewhere on a preserved railway. In consequence, the number of visitors declined.

The Museum's road vehicles attended rallies and participated in events such as the *Trans- Pennine Run* from Manchester to Harrogate and the *Blackpool to Southport Run*. These activities compensated in some measure for the lack of progress made on the railway restoration front. The August 1978 newsletter mused how much better things might have been if the 1,000 or so people starting off as ELRPS members over the last decade or so had all stayed the course. As it was, membership tended to reach about 200 each year but then taper off at renewal time in the absence of progress made towards railway operation.

New Transport Interchange

In 1978, a grant of £1,000 came from the *Greater Manchester Council* to repair the Museum roof. In that same year, an announcement was made that the Manchester to Bury electric trains would be diverted from Bolton Street to a new bus and rail Transport Interchange station sited alongside *Kay Gardens* in Bury. With construction completed in March 1980, remaining passenger services switched to the new station with Bury Bolton Street being closed.

Meanwhile, the last electric train had left Bury Bolton Street on 14 March 1980. The tracks were realigned over the weekend so that from Monday morning, trains from Manchester left the old route at *Loco Junction*, travelling a short way along the *Bury Loop* before curving sharply onto a new alignment leading to the island platform adjacent to the *Bus Interchange*. The new line sliced through the derelict platform at Bury Knowsley Street (the station had been demolished in 1971), crossing on the level at right angles the remaining single track which carried the coal trains from Castleton via Bury to Rawtenstall.

Termination of coal trains

New possibilities opened up for the ELRPS following an announcement that the coal train schedule to and from Rawtenstall was to cease operation. Whilst the demise of BR's last tenuous involvement in Rossendale shut one door, it very much opened up another for the Society. The decision to close the coal line to Rawtenstall came on the back of a dramatically reduced demand for the fuel. Although, up to the 60s, coal had been the main fuel source for manufacturing businesses and also for heating domestic properties, gas usage had taken its place, with demand soaring through the 70s.

The depot at Rawtenstall had capacity to handle 80,000 tons of coal per annum, being brought on site by train and then distributed around the Rossendale valley via road transport. The trains were hauled by diesel locomotives - steam traction having been withdrawn from the rail network in 1968 - with the most common model used being *Class 25s* and *40s*. However, the frequency of coal trains was now down to just once a week.

'By the late 1970s, there were only one or two desultory diesels with a dozen trucks crawling up the line once or twice a week delivering coal to Rawtenstall. They only stopped at Ramsbottom whilst the signal boxes were unlocked by the crew so that the crossing gates could be opened and closed. An air of decrepitude and imminent mortality hung over the branch.' [1]

The final coal train to Rawtenstall ran on 5 December 1980, over eight years after passenger services had ended, with *No. 40098* given the honour of being the final locomotive to haul a freight train along the remaining section of line through Heywood, Bury and Ramsbottom before terminating at Rawtenstall.

Rossendale Farewell Railtour

On Saturday 14 February 1981, the evocative sight of a passenger train had re-appeared on line, courtesy of a '*Rossendale Farewell Railtour*' plying its way from Manchester Victoria to Rawtenstall via Heywood and Bury. Using a six-coach *DMU*, the event had been organised by Rossendale-based rail enthusiast David Isherwood with a ticket price of £9.50. The train paused en route at Bury Bolton Street on the outward journey so that the 300 passengers could visit the *Transport Museum*.

The same month also witnessed the first ex-BR main line diesel locomotives, Western Region diesel-hydraulics *D832 'Onslaught'* and *D1041 'Western Prince',* being delivered by rail to Castlecroft. These two new arrivals were accommodated in a newly-constructed three-road shed at the bottom of the yard, alongside the Bury to Rawtenstall line.

The Society had wasted no time in launching a '*Save The Line Appeal*'. At the most basic level, a donation of £1 entitled the donor to one free journey whilst at the other end of the spectrum, a £1,000 commitment provided the donor with a free pass for life. The harsh reality though was that, despite twelve years of fund-raising, the Society was in no stronger position to purchase the Bury-Rawtenstall line than it had been to acquire the Helmshore route back in 1968. None of this though stopped the Society from continuing to pursue its aims. If anything, the never-say-die spirit grew stronger amongst hard-core members.

Mindful of the importance of the Bolton Street site to any future Bury-Rawtenstall operation, the Society sought to gain assurances from local authorities that it was not about to be demolished. A meeting took place on 19 March 1981 involving representatives of the Society, BR and Greater Manchester, Lancashire, Bury and Rossendale Councils, at which it was agreed that BR would protect the site and postpone lifting the track-line until at least August, allowing discussions to continue.

There was no doubt that Council perceptions were beginning to change at this stage and that railway preservation was now being seen as a potentially valuable tourist trade amenity. On another bright note, increased levels of rail activity had seen Society membership climbing to 350 by the middle of 1981.

The Phoenix rises: 1982 onwards

In an attempt to convince the local authorities that there was a demand for its proposed rail service, the Society successfully chartered a special weekend event on the Bury to Rawtenstall line on 27/28 March 1982. The event took place on the same date as the official closing of the original line had done ten years earlier. During these two days, an eight-car *DMU* ran three times from Bury Bolton Street to Rawtenstall.

The first departure took place at 10.30 am on the Saturday to the strains of *'See the Conquering Hero Comes'*, the music that had welcomed the first ELR train to Bury in 1846. There were two coaches reserved for guests including councillors, council officers, BR officials and representatives of the *North West Tourist Board*. The event had witnessed the appearance of ex-Manchester Ship Canal

0-6-0T 70, officially named '*Phoenix*' for the purpose of the initiative. A total of 1,300 passengers travelled the route on the Saturday whilst more than 2,000 people were reported to have visited the museum.

During 1983, the Society gained permission to alter the track lay-out at Bury Bolton Street. There were further deliveries of rolling stock including two further main line diesels: *class 35 'Hymek' No. D7076* and *class 24 No. D5054*. A number of coaches were also purchased, as the railway steadily kept on gearing itself up for the time when it might be able to operate a proper service of its own. A '*Grand Transport Extravaganza*' was arranged over the Spring Bank Holiday with permission given by BR to display locomotives and rolling stock in Bolton Street station.

Successful purchasing of the line

Significant breakthrough came about on 9 November 1983 when the Greater Manchester Council, with Rossendale Council's approval, granted that the Bury to Rawtenstall line should be re-opened as a heritage line/tourist amenity. The key enabling factor was the so-called '*Derelict Land Grant*' which presented Greater Manchester and Rossendale with the longer-term opportunity to receive from Central Government as much as £1.2 million out of their projected overall £1.7 million costs supporting the project. The successful purchasing of the line undoubtedly came on the back of grant funding. In Spring 1984, the Department for the Environment directly awarded a *Derelict Land Grant* of £435,000 to Greater Manchester Council and Rossendale Council to fund the purchase of the line from BR.

Other encouraging signs came when private owner groups approached the Company asking for permission to bring their locos to Bury. For example, in February 1984, *40 40145* arrived to be followed in May by 45337, one of the famous *Black Fives* built in 1937 by the LMS.

Happily, the two Councils consented to the purchase and then sanctioned a lease of the line for a period of 90 years to the East Lancashire Railway Trust – a body endowed with charitable status. The Board of nine was to consist of three members each from Greater

Manchester, Rossendale Councils and the East Lancashire Railway Company.

The ELR Trust was to administer the funds for the restoration and development of the railway. The Trust leased the line and property from the local authorities which then leased on to the East Lancashire Light Railway Company.The ELLRCo was to be responsible for the day-to-day running of the railway and was the formal legal structure under which the Society worked. For its part, the ELRPS's members went on providing the volunteer labour force to cover the operation and maintenance of the railway plus a variety of other services such as publicity, catering and sales.

Meanwhile, it was boldly announced in the Winter/Spring 1984 edition of the *Bury Transport Museum Journal* that 'the Bury-Ramsbottom Line Re-opens Spring 1985'. However, in early 1986, complications arose with regard to a regulation called the '*Light Railway Order*'. This needed to be passed before the Society could be granted the right to operate services. The purchase of the railway from BR was not yet completed before the process became further complicated following news that Greater Manchester Council was soon to be abolished. Given that the GMC had been so supportive to date, this was far from welcome news.

Speaking more recently with Keith Whitmore, who was chairing the *GM Passenger Transport Authority* at the time, the impending abolition of the council strengthened general resolve to do as much as possible to push forward the heritage line's cause in the short time left. Thankfully, most of GMC's functions in this direction ended up being devolved to the Metropolitan Borough of Bury Council which endorsed the Society's core objectives.

Another *Derelict Land Grant* was awarded during the course of 1986 to Bury and Rossendale Councils, this time for £600,000. The money was provided to enable structures along the line to be restored to acceptable standards of working practice. Following years of neglect, the line was in a run-down condition. For example, four bridges needed to be replaced between Ramsbottom and Rawtenstall whilst the stations themselves at both those locations were virtually non-existent by now. The argument seemed irrefutable that the line had by this stage degenerated into 'derelict land'.

By Autumn 1986, all of the legal paperwork had been completed and 'Bury-Rawtenstall' was formally signed over from BR and the line then leased to East Lancashire Light Railway Co. Limited. After 18 years and countless setbacks, the ELRPS and its army of volunteers could justifiably feel confident that the company's core ambition was on the cusp of being achieved.

Further work needing to be carried out

Many practical requirements still needed addressing though. Volunteers had their work cut out for example stabilising an area just to the south of Summerseat station which had a historic problem with landslips. It was not until Saturday 27 December 1986 that the *Sentinel* shunter, the works train venturing up the line as far as Summerseat, was able to undertake the remedial trackwork necessary to enable driver training and familiarisation runs to take place.

Contractors had been hired to drain Square Reservoir viaduct just south of Ramsbottom, replacing it with a plain embankment. Meanwhile, the installation of the points and crossings forming the loops at Bury and Ramsbottom was taken on by the Society's volunteer force with a helping hand from a *Manpower Services Commission* team.

The Signalling Engineering Department, led by Peter Duncan, carried out installation of signalling at Bury and Ramsbottom. At the same time, making Ramsbottom station fit for purpose called for a lot of work, for example having its long-neglected platform re-flagged as well as being extended by a further two lengths to allow six coaches to be accommodated. A run round loop was constructed alongside the platform. The longer-term need for level crossing and signal box was deferred until the line should come to be extended to Rawtenstall. A temporary portable building was put up, containing a waiting room, toilets and a small booking office. Further facilities were to follow later, including the installation of a water tower.

The ELR Locomotive and Carriage & Wagon Department had carried out considerable work from 1985 onwards, for example subjecting certain engines, including ex-Central Electricity Gas Board (*CEGB) 'No. 1'* and *'Bickershaw'*, to rigorous examination and repair. The privately-owned *'Gothenburg'* received similar attention.

'Gothenburg'

The steam engine had a most interesting history. Built in 1903, it had originally been owned by the Manchester Ship Canal Company who named their early engines after places that ships from the port traded with. However, in 1915, following the sinking of the *Lusitania* during World War I, anti-German feeling had run so high that the company decided to strip all German-sounding names from locos. This was despite the fact that the city of Gothenburg actually is in Sweden! It had not been until 1976 that the loco was given back its original name. A new *'Gothenburg'* plate was struck and an official re-naming ceremony was held which was attended by the Swedish Consul based in the UK.

Owned by Ian Riley, he had bought the engine for £3,000 in 1980 off a fellow rail enthusiast who himself had brought it to the transport museum's yard in 1976. For the past seven years, Ian had painstakingly restored, rebuilt and renovated the engine to her former glory. 'In those days, I was an engineer at our family firm in Heywood where we worked on mill engines so I felt I knew what I was doing.' [2]

Overhaul of Diesels

As well as the above steam engines, several diesel locomotives also underwent serious overhaul, involving the removal, restoration and replacement of power units. Of the diesel-electrics, the *Class 24* was in good condition when received and only required a general clean-up whereas more detailed work was necessary on the *Class 40* group. A knock-on task facing the Carriage & Wagon team followed the substitution of a number of coach bogies under an exchange deal with BR in 1985/6. The refurbishment of carriage interiors, renovation of bodywork involved considerable input from the volunteer team. The combined rolling stock would form the basis for the pending first season of operation, although there were further coaches and locomotives being lined up for use at a later date.

A few last delays encountered

Despite the tremendous effort put in, opening-date targets continued to slide. For example it was stated in the Society newsletter for November/December that the line would re-open on 6 June. However, following a visit from Major Olver of the Railway Inspectorate in April, it had been recommended that the reopening date be put back until the end of July.

Over the Spring Bank Holiday, the annual vehicle cavalcade took place to Rawtenstall and back while Bolton Street station and the Museum were once again the setting for a *Grand Transport Extravaganza*. Significantly, this though marked the last occasion on which the Society had to rely on road vehicles and static exhibits for a prestige annual event.

Re-opening of ELR line from Bury to Ramsbottom on 25 July 1987

Over fifteen years had elapsed since passenger services were withdrawn from the Bury to Rawtenstall line back on 3 June 1972 and nearly seven since the last coal train had passed along the line on 5 December 1980. The long anticipated 're-opening' eventually came about on the morning of Saturday 25 July. Preparations got underway when the two steam locomotives, ELR *'No. 1'* and *'Gothenburg'* double-headed a train consisting of six maroon *Mark One* coaches from Buckley Wells to Bury Bolton Street station. The driver of *ELR 'No. 1'* was Phil Southern, whilst Ian Riley drove his own *'Gothenburg'*.

At Bury, 339 invited guests and dignitaries had been welcomed at the main entrance by Station Master Harry Hatcher before assembling on platform 3 and 4. Entertainment to mark the big day was provided by the *Irwell Forge Band*. At 10.20 a.m., the Mayor of Bury, Councillor Mrs Jacqui Adler arrived to be welcomed by Trevor Jones, Chairman of the EL Light Railway. Also present on the occasion was Mayor of Rossendale, Councillor Patrick Navin.

After the Mayor of Bury and Trevor Jones had addressed guests, Councillor Adler signalled the train to run into platform 3. At 11 a.m., the Mayor gave the 'right away' with green flag and whistle from the vestibule-door of the leading vehicle. To the strains of the band

– and tumultuous cheering – the train embarked on its historic five-mile journey to Ramsbottom.

Arrival of the train in Ramsbottom

The train arrived at Ramsbottom at 11.20 a.m., breaking through a celebratory banner strung across the platform. On alighting from their carriages, passengers were treated to musical renditions from the '*Clan Grant Pipe Band*' hailing from Grantown-on-Spey, situated about twenty miles south of Inverness in Scotland, the original stamping ground of Ramsbottom's illustrious Grant family, who had lived there before migrating south to East Lancashire before becoming prominent figures in Ramsbottom..

The Bury-Ramsbottom link was further emphasised on the day by the coming together on the platform of respective Station Masters, Ramsbottom's Dave Greenwood and Bury's legendary ELR stalwart, Harry Hatcher. Two vintage open-top cars conducted leading guests up Bridge Street to a Chamber of Trade welcoming ceremony at the *Old Market Place* where the *Ramsbottom Steam Jazz Band* struck up a welcoming musical rendition. Dignitaries were then escorted back to the railway station to board the return train to Bury, setting off at 12.10. Lunch was provided at the *Castle Leisure Centre.*

The day was blessed with good weather throughout. A number of celebratory events had been put on in Ramsbottom such as a balloon race at midday. Also, there were charity displays and stalls in the market square and station car park. A fun fair was held in *Nuttall Park* and various activities took place at *Holcombe Hill* with the *Peel Monument* open for visitors during the day.

Further passenger trains left Bury at 1.30 pm, 3.00 pm, 4.30 pm and 6 pm. Whilst the first three were reserved for VIPs, later carriages were available for members of the public with tickets needing to have been purchased in advance at £5. In the evening, a free celebratory service was organised for the benefit of volunteers and members of the ELRPS, departing from Bury at 8.00 pm. More than 250 people made this trip to Ramsbottom. On the way back, the train stopped off at Summerseat for passengers to partake of an evening buffet at the *Waterside Inn*, provided by Society President Les Ratcliffe.

On the next day, although the weather was not as good, demand for train seats on the schedule was so great that an extra service was put on. The *Bury Times* quoted Trevor Jones, Chairman of the ELR, commenting on the success of the weekend as a whole: 'All the way along, we knew people appreciated the chance to have a service of this kind and wanted it. That has certainly been proved to be the case. It was just fantastic.' [3]

§

Influence of Trevor Jones on the development of the ELR

Through the strength of his commitment to the ELR, Trevor Jones had every right to feel elated on the occasion of the re-opening of the line. Born in 1945 into a railway family, Trevor's grandfather had been a signalman at Townsend Fold whilst his father had worked at Bacup Junction Box, later moving to Ramsbottom and then to Smithy Bridge near Rochdale. It was here in the late 50s that Trevor made the acquaintance of Richard Greenwood who was later to become counterpart Chairman of the Worth Valley Company. As youngsters, they had both frequented Smithy Bridge Box when Trevor's father was on duty.

Trevor had been tempted to join the Worth Valley but had instead joined the East Lancashire Society upon its formation in 1968. There had been many frustrations along the way which caused other early members to abandon the project. He had kept faith though throughout. When the first sign of breakthrough had come in 1980 following closure of Bolton Street station and withdrawal of the coal line to Rawtenstall, Trevor had sought to enter into partnership with neighbouring local authorities to keep ambitions fuelled.

In the midst of a deep recession, during which traditional industries were suffering massive decline, Trevor remained acutely aware of the need for local government to support initiatives aimed at turning the general economic situation around. A salesman by occupation, he proved a persuasive voice in advocating the potential of the ELR to play a key role as a tourist attraction. In more practical terms, he and others around him had spared no effort in seeking to tap in to the resources, such as financial grants, available to bid for during this period.

As to what it meant to Trevor personally, after having long ago become chairman of the railway company charged with the task of restoring the line, he later recalled: 'Twenty years ago we had 40 members and 80 feet of track and we were collecting waste paper to raise money. We've come a long way since then and we are going further with the new line and new stations. It brought home to me a bit back on a certain trip to London when I stood on Euston station and saw our train to Ramsbottom up on the board with all the main line services. I felt it was showing to the world that we were doing our bit. It brought a lump to my throat I can tell you.' [4]

Boost to Ramsbottom from the re-opening of the railway

Ramsbottom had been in the doldrums for years, suffering the effects of the severe economic downturn that had befallen East Lancashire towns in the wake of the decline of traditional industries such as cotton. During the 70s and 80s, the town, like many others in East Lancashire had taken on a run-down appearance, characterised by disused mills and boarded-up shops. Against this background, a new sense of optimism emerged with regard to the revitalising effect the restored railway service might have on the fortunes of the town.

Mrs Barbara Palmer, President of the *Ramsbottom Chamber of Trade*, remarked: 'It is very much an experimental year as far as the railway and Ramsbottom goes but this seems an easy and ideal way to promote the area. A boom in tourism centred on the town may seem a novel idea but it is not impossible.' [5]

Following the re-opening of the line, the ELR was keen to move things forward on its own account. One planned-for initiative was '*Santa Specials*' – trains to run at Christmas aimed amongst other things at enticing shoppers to Ramsbottom. '*Santa Specials*' took place through December with a gift from Father Christmas for all children a main feature of the occasion. Over 8,000 passengers participated in the seasonal treat.

By the end of the year, 35,000 people had travelled along the four-mile long Bury-Ramsbottom track. One interesting side-effect had been the number of people from Ramsbottom who used the service the other way to go shopping in Bury. This phenomenon caused the local bus operation, *GM Buses*, to reduce its fares between Ramsbottom and Bury from £1.50 to £1.10 in face of the new competition.

The ELR fleet

The mainstay of motive power in those early days was ex-CEGB *0-6-0T No. 1*, purchased from Meaford Power Station near Stone, Staffordshire, and No. 32 *Gothenburg*. Other 'industrials' in the fleet included North Western Gas Board *0-4-0ST No. 1* (AB 1927/27) and ex-NCB '*Austerity*' 0-6-0ST No. 8 *Bickershaw* (Hunslet 3776/52), renamed *Sir Robert Peel* by the ELR.

The company's diesel fleet included 'Warship' Class No. D832 *Onslaught*, 'Western' Class *No D1041 Western Prince*, '*Hymek*' *No. D7076*, and *Class 40 No. 40145*, as well as several industrial diesels. Coaching stock was made up of ex-BR *Mark 1s*, which were being repaired to early-1960s-style maroon livery. [6]

ELR Spreads its Wings

The idea of conducting 'railtours' came about soon after when, on 19 September 1987, the ELR line ran a train from Ramsbottom to Carlisle. *ELR 'No. 1'* hauled the nine-coach train from Ramsbottom to Bury before a BR locomotive took over for the onward leg of the tour. Another innovative step was adopted on 7 November 1987 with the Southern Electric Group organising a tour from London Euston, given the heading '*East Lancashire Executive*'. This was the first charter excursion train that had journeyed from the British Rail network onto the ELR line since it had re-opened to passengers in July.

Upon arrival at Bury Bolton Street, the *BR Class 47* gave way to ELR traction, with *D832* and *40145* operating either side of the ten-coach train, *D832* leading from Bury to Ramsbottom. Passengers were able to spend time exploring Ramsbottom before returning to Bury, with *40145* leading the return working. Beyond this point, the railtour made its way back down the Bury to Manchester line. The tour also took in a selection of other local lines en route before heading back to London Euston. It had proved a successful venture all-round and one which demonstrated ELR's capacity to play host to incoming railtours whilst at the same time offering an interesting addition to the Company's core schedule of events.

ELRPS wins prestigious award

1987 had proved a highly successful year, at the end of which Society membership had risen in excess of 1,000 for the first time. New Year 1988 got off to a flying start with it being announced that the ELRPS had won the prestigious *Association of Railway Preservation Societies (ARPS)* annual award in recognition of the re-opening of the railway between Bury and Ramsbottom in July 1987. The award, an impressive framed royal coat of arms, once carried by locomotives hauling the *Royal Train* (owned by the National Railway Museum in York, but loaned to the ARPS), was presented to the ELRPS at the Association's Annual General Meeting in Manchester on 30 January 1988. During 1988, the number of passengers travelling on the railway rose dramatically to 60,000 from the previous year's figure of 35,000.

New station improvements at Ramsbottom

Meanwhile, necessary work was carried out along the line. With the next ELR goal in mind to extend the line to Rawtenstall, the company recognised it needed to carry out a major programme of improvements to facilities at Ramsbottom station. Firstly, a new water tower was erected to assist powering steam locomotives working on the railway. Capable of holding 2,500 gallons of water, the fabrication work was carried out by volunteers Ian Riley and Alan Schofield. The new water tower was moved to Ramsbottom by train, with a crane brought in to lift the tower into position on the platform.

This installation was the first of several measures put into place on site including re-flagging the surviving platform, as well as extending it by a further two coach lengths to allow six coach trains to be comfortably accommodated on track. Building work on the new permanent station started in 1988 at a cost of £90,000. Employing a team of 14 builders, the project (after the original builder had gone bankrupt) came subsequently to be assigned to local businessman Fred Rothwell who commented: 'This contract means a lot to us, especially as this is my home town.' [7]

Given that Ramsbottom town centre was now accessible to tourists travelling by rail, there was also need to offer ways and means of promoting other nearby attractions. The fact that not all of these were within walking distance of the railway led to the establishment of a connecting bus service. In 1988, Rossendale Transport Limited gained the Greater Manchester PTE contract to operate the 476 '*Ramsbottom Rover*' service between Ramsbottom station and *Helmshore Textile Museum/Clough Head Quarry*, via Holcombe Village.

The re-opened railway station received the official stamp of approval in a civic ceremony on 19 June 1989, officially opened by 'His Worship the Mayor of Bury Metropolitan Borough, Councillor Alan Matthews'. Designed by Bury Council architect, Steven Lever, the re-created site was built in a style as sympathetic as possible to that of original ELR engineer John Shae Perring going back to the 1840s. It featured an entrance hall, shop, booking office and kitchen area, a waiting room together with toilet facilities. Subsequently, 'society officials were delighted to learn that Ramsbottom station had been "*Highly Commended*" by the judges in the *1989 Ian Allan Railway Heritage Awards*'. [8]

Bearing in mind plans to extend the line to Rawtenstall, work started on making Ramsbottom suitable for its new role as a 'through station' with provision made for two platforms, full signalling, and a loop for trains to pass each other. Between 8 and 10 July, a road closure had been put in place on Bridge Street to allow the rails over the level crossing to be replaced and the road re-surfaced to reinstate the level crossing for double-track operations. Ducting and signal cabling was simultaneously installed beneath the crossing, successfully completed in time for the road to be re-opened according to schedule. The second platform was built later in the year and the iron footbridge (which had transferred from the *Dinting Railway Centre* in Glossop, following its closure) installed between Christmas and the New Year with the aid of a 50-ton steam crane to place it imposingly over the track.

More Progress Down the Line

In 1988, it was brought to public notice that the Bury to Manchester electric railway line was to be replaced by a new Metrolink scheme. Ominously, the new development threatened to have an adverse effect in terms of isolating the ELR from the national rail network, with the platforms along the Metrolink route having to be altered to accommodate the new light rail vehicles, making them unsuitable for the passage of standard railway rolling stock.

However, an alternative opportunity opened up to the ELR based on potential use of a stretch of line between Heywood and Bury. Part of the former Rochdale-Bolton, until it had closed to passenger services in October 1970, the line had been used by freight trains conveying coal to Rawtenstall until the end of 1980. A single line had remained in place in the meantime. Most of this appeared to be still in reasonably good condition.

At Heywood, the *Standard Wagon Works* was still active, with trains running to its works from Castleton. It was estimated that the derelict line running through Bury towards Rawtenstall could be restored at a relatively modest cost of £350,000. As well as obtaining support for the project from Bury Council, ELR was further encouraged by backing given by Rochdale Council.

Other encouraging news came in June when *Class 25 diesel locomotive 25909* was delivered to Bury to join the railway's growing fleet of diesel locomotives. Owned by TV personality and record producer Pete Waterman, the locomotive had been purchased from BR in good condition. It was to make a notable contribution to the ELR's first '*Diesel Weekend*' which was held over 1/2 October 1988. The occasion proved both popular and profitable, showing that there was a strong market for events aimed at diesel enthusiasts. It was also to mark the start of a valuable and longstanding association between the ELR and passionate rail enthusiast Pete Waterman.

Less positive news however came in early February 1989 when it was announced that the planned opening of a passenger rail line to

Rawtenstall, scheduled to take place during the August 1989 Bank Holiday weekend, was now postponed until at least Easter 1990. One reason for the delay was a series of modifications needing to be carried out to bring two other level crossings back into use – at Townsend Fold and Rawtenstall West. While this work was still underway, there also remained a number of other projects to be completed, such as the installation of replacement river bridges between Irwell Vale and Ewood Bridge, together with another on the approach to Rawtenstall.

Opening of Irwell Vale 'Halt'

The ELR decision taken to construct a 'halt' at Irwell Vale, en route from Ramsbottom to Rawtenstall, was based on providing a gateway to the surrounding countryside for hikers and ramblers. On 1 May 1989, the ELR hosted an *Irwell Valley Adventure* launch event, with Winter Olympic ski jumper Eddie '*The Eagle*' Edwards and Pete Waterman featuring as celebrity attractions. Local radio personality Susie Mathis hosted the day, with the site's new mascot, '*Irwell the Cat*' providing more zany input.

Irwell Vale's location was distinctive for the fact it was connected by road from a single road direction only, that from Ewood Bridge. Reaching Irwell Vale, the motor-road goes no further. In present day times, it was hard to visualise that the sleepy hamlet had once been *'a child of the Industrial Revolution'* (as an information board relates) and a centre of commerce with a thriving settlement around it, boasting three mills, two chapels, a post office and a co-op shop.

As described in an earlier chapter, Thomas Aitken, a cotton manufacturer who owned mills in Chatterton and Irwell Vale towards the middle of the 19th century, had been amongst the group of pioneering industrialists convening at the *Red Lion* in Bury in 1843 to push forward the case for a rail link-up joining up Manchester, Bury and Rossendale. John Bowker was also a local mill-owner who played a part in linking up Irwell Vale to the 'old-ER' Bury to Rawtenstall line of 1846. Bowker's first mill had been built on Hardsough Lane, adjacent to where the railway line now runs through Irwell Vale.

Although both these mill-owners' factories have since been demolished, their names still resonate with the two main thoroughfares in Irwell Vale being named *Bowker Street* and *Aitken Street.* Also redolent of the past are the neat rows of cottages, standing along these streets, built originally for mill workers. On a property standing at the corner of Bowker and Aitken Streets, the year '*1833*' is etched on an upper-floor wall. Albeit renovated in recent times, the former workers' cottages have certainly stood the test of time. Enjoying conservation area rights, the dwellings have been designated Grade II-protected status.

The new station at Irwell Vale was completed and handed over to the ELR by Lancashire County Council on 28 September 1989. On the day, the event, as shown on BBC local news programme *North West Tonight*, featured the arrival there of a train top-and-tailed by Derek Foster's *76079* and *Class 47, D1842*, loaned for the purpose from its base at *Crewe Heritage Centre.*

Further promising signs for the future

Another notable ELR innovation happened later in the year when, on a warm and sunny Bank Holiday on Monday 28 August 1989, a '*Teddy Bear's Picnic*' took place at *Nuttall Park* in Ramsbottom, offering a variety of family-friendly rides and attractions. An added enticement was that all children accompanied by a teddy bear (and a fare-paying adult) travelled free of charge between Bury and Ramsbottom. Success on the day ensured that *Nuttall Park* would continue to host this perennially-popular event in following years.

Later on in the year, encouraging findings emerged from a detailed feasibility study launched by Bury and Rochdale Councils aimed at evaluating the economic value of reinstating the line from Bury to Heywood. Positive outcomes from the exercise led to both Councils expressing support for an extension proposal.

Allowing for certain frustrations along the way, the 1980s had ended very successfully for the ELR across several fronts. Despite obvious challenges lying ahead, there still seemed every reason to look forward optimistically to the 1990s.

Notes

1. Andrew Todd – Foreword to Vol 1 of *Ramsbottom Reminiscences* (1992) p.7
2. *Bury Times Rail Commemorative Special*, 24 July 1987
3. *Bury Times*, 28 June 1987
4. *Lancashire Life*, September 1988
5. *Bury Times*, 1 May 1987
6. David Mather, *East Lancashire Railway Recollections* (2015) Silver Link Publishing Ltd. p. 5
7. *Bury Times*, 13 January 1988
8. *Rossendale Free Press*, 3 November 1989

Chapter Nine – Rolling on to Rawtenstall

ELR adds to its events calendar

On 24 April 1990, the Annual General Meeting of the ELRPS took place in the function room above the *Waterside Inn* at Summerseat. Harry Hatcher, having given stout service as Society Chairman (1970-2 and 1978-90), stood down with Tony Wright being voted into the role. Another change involved Dave Russell finishing as Secretary to be replaced by Lois Vevers, wife of Treasurer Graham.

In February, *Murder on the Ramsbottom Express* was acted out on a train travelling from Bury to Ramsbottom. Inspired by Agatha Christie's famous railway mystery, the event was staged by re-enactors, dressed in 1920s fashions. 'One of the more unusual charters in recent times required the provision of a body, a bottle of tomato ketchup and numerous pens and notepads. The theme was that a murder had been committed on the train and the remaining passengers had to solve who had done it'. [1]

On 4 May, the ELR operated its first ever dining train with the company's promotion of the '*The Presidential Diner*'. Catering was provided by '*Bury College Caterers*' students and staff, with ELR volunteers serving wine and drinks to diners. Priced at £15.50 per person, inclusive of wine, the menu offered starters of pink grapefruit or prawns and salad. The main course was chicken breast stuffed with Parma ham and avocado with spring vegetables and new potatoes. For desserts, it was strawberry tartlet and cream, cheese and biscuits, and coffee. The occasion proved so successful that work began on the restoration of a *Mark 1 SO* carriage for future events. The new facility would boast umber and cream livery, in similar style to Pullman.

In June, the ELR launched its first midweek train service with a '*Schools Week*', taking place 12-14 June. The three days were designed to provide local children with a rail-ride experience and also visit nearby attractions. The itinerary was organised between the railway and local councils with input also from *Helmshore Textiles Museum* and *Rossendale Groundwork Trust.* [2]

'Thomas – A Tank for All Seasons'

A vexed question during these times was whether to stage a '*Thomas the Tank Engine*' event or not. Malcolm Vickers expressed the dilemma: 'Previously held views on the ELR were that Thomas and everything associated with the Rev. W. Awdry's railway series was "not for us" as an authentic preserved railway set in the late 50s/early 60s. The subject was raised again at the June council meeting. This came in response to Brian Topping's repeated exhortations regarding the need for more events which would stimulate better attendance by the public'.

Over the weekend of 22/23 September, the railway did in fact host its first '*Thomas the Tank Engine and Friends*' weekend. The former Meaford Power Station *0-6-OT ELR 'No. 1'* took the role of Thomas. In subsequent years, ex-Manchester Ship Canal *0-6-0 32*, the inimitable '*Gothenburg*' was painted into Thomas' blue livery to play the part of the popular children's train-engine character.

Despite Saturday proving a mixed day weather-wise, Malcolm Vickers reported 'it did not deter the visitors who came in their droves. By mid-afternoon, Bolton Street platforms 3 and 4 were packed with knowledgeable boys and girls, with mums and dads who had come to assess the quality and authenticity of the ELR *Thomas the Tank* offering'.

One or two hiccups though: 'Not one, but many small souls castigated the '*Fat Controller*' for not wearing a yellow (instead of grey) waistcoat; we'll get it right next time! However, notwithstanding that small, but apparently important detail, everyone seemed to be entering into the spirit of the occasion, with the peddlers of Thomas tank engines, flags, whistles and other paraphernalia doing a roaring trade'.

Proving a resounding success, all bar one of ELR's operational steam locomotives had been in service, together with the running of three diesels. 'The station, operational and catering staff, loco crews and the public all reported that they had thoroughly enjoyed themselves. The booking office staff were also smiling with passenger numbers at 5,349, a record for a single weekend, proving that, indeed, Thomas is "A Tank for All Seasons" '.[3]

'Just William Day'

On 17 November, the ELR organised a *'Just William Day'* in association with *Bury Metro Events.* Richmal Crompton (1890-1969), the author of the *'Just William'* books - about a mischievous 11-year-old schoolboy and his band of friends, known as *'The Outlaws'* - was born in Bury. The event coincided with the centenary of her birth. Children and adults were encouraged to dress as characters from the books and this event also went very well.

Opening of Ramsbottom to Rawtenstall line: 27 April 1991

The New Year into 1991 had heralded the start of two-train operations as the ELR geared up for re-opening through to Rawtenstall. The commissioning of the signalling, level crossing and extended run-round facilities at Ramsbottom at the end of 1990 enabled trains to pass at the station for the first time. The running of two trains required ELR to fine-tune timetable details and also train staff to become used to operating trains on the new sections of line. Although the restoration of the Ramsbottom to Rawtenstall section of the railway had not been without its problems and missed opening dates, the end target now lay within practical reach.

After a set of familiarisation trips for training purposes, the long-awaited re-opening took place on Saturday 27 April 1991. The weather was fine and bright as the immaculately clean six-coach train, hauled by *0-6-OT 32 'Gothenburg'* and *0-6-OT ELR 'No. 1'* pulled into Platform 3 at Bury Bolton Street station, bursting through a celebratory banner stretched across the track. *32* was crewed by Terry Whitehouse and John Lewis, with Joe Strickleton and Malcolm Frost crewing *ELR 'No. 1'*. As in 1987, the serving Mayor of Bury was called upon to wave off the first train. By coincidence, it happened to be Councillor Monty Adler, husband of Councillor Jacqui Adler who had been Mayor of Bury when the official opening of the line to Ramsbottom had taken place four years earlier.

The train arrived at Ramsbottom where it was greeted by the *Haslingden and Helmshore Brass Band.* There was a scheduled 17-minute stop at the station, allowing time for various speeches and the topping-up of the two engines' water tanks. Meanwhile, the Mayor of Bury and his Rossendale counterpart, Councillor Philip Dunne, unveiled a plaque at Ramsbottom station to commemorate the opening to Rawtenstall.

After departure from Ramsbottom, the train made its way to Rawtenstall, where another banner had been placed across the tracks to be broken through. The train was greeted tumultuously by hundreds of enthusiasts who had arrived to witness the event. Station master Dave Russell, having previously carried out the same role at Ramsbottom, was on hand to welcome the train and the dignitaries aboard. The *Water Brass Band* played the train into the station before vintage buses ferried guests to *The Astoria* for lunch.

Following the return of the celebratory re-opening train to Bury, an hourly service operated through the rest of the afternoon, with *32* and *ELR 'No. 1'* hauling the maroon six-coach train. Meanwhile, Derek Foster's *BR Standard 4 76079* and *Ken Ryder's 7828 'Odney Manor'* took turns to be in charge of the second train, consisting of five carmine and cream *Mark One* coaches. By the end of the year, the opening to Rawtenstall had proved to be extremely popular, with an 85% increase in passengers travelling on the railway in 1991 compared to the previous year. [4]

More pulling power required

The extension to Rawtenstall, involving the hauling of longer trains up still more testing gradients, caused the company to have to add to its stock of locomotives, including two LMS '*Black 5s*', Nos. 44871 and 45407, LMS '*Crab*' 2-6-0 No. 42765, GWR 2-8-0 No. 3855 and 2-8-2T No. 7229, SR '*Battle of Britain*' Class No. 34073 249 *Squadron* and *Merchant Navy* no. 35009 *Shaw Savill*, LNER 'B 12/2' 4-6-0 No. 61572, and the unique BR 8P 'Pacific' No. 71000 *Duke of Gloucester.* [5]

§

Film cameras roll

Another first for the company came in 1991 in the form of providing a film set for Pinewood Studios. The title was *'Let Him Have It'*, featuring Christopher Eccleston, Paul Reynolds, Eileen Atkins and Tom Courtenay, telling the story of Derek Bentley, a young man who had been hanged after being found guilty of shooting a policeman following a controversial court case in 1953.

The film contained railway scenes which were recorded close to Bury EL Tunnel. Other scenes were filmed in and around Bury, despite the location of the crime having in true life taken place in Croydon in the south of England. *'Let Him Have It'* was the first of many instances of film companies looking to the ELR to provide a railway setting for their productions.

Planning approval gained for the Heywood Extension

On 13 February 1992, an official planning application for re-establishing the line from Heywood to Bury was submitted to Rochdale Council's Planning Committee. The motion to proceed with the project was carried with six votes in favour and none against. Still waiting for the statutory powers to be transferred by BR, it was recognised that it would take some time before passenger trains were able to start serving the area again.

Rawtenstall's new station opens

A ceremony took place on 16 April 1992 to commemorate the re-opening of Rawtenstall station. It was conducted by Rossendale Mayor, Councillor Graham Pearson. The L-shaped station building, costing £250,000, was positioned at the end of the platforms, partially covering over where trains had once sped on to Bacup.

The new station included a spacious booking hall, booking office, gift shop, waiting room and toilet facilities. A special feature was the impressive clock tower above the booking hall, which was similar in appearance to the one which had stood over the original entrance area at Bury Bolton Street station up to the time that the ground-level site had been destroyed by fire in 1947. A special train was commissioned for invited guests travelling between Bury and Rawtenstall in honour of the occasion, with *Standard 4 76069* being chosen for the purpose.

Pete Waterman invests more heavily in *Class 50* diesels

Rail enthusiast Pete Waterman's collection of locomotives and rolling stock was growing considerably at this time. During 1992, he bought two *Class 50* diesel locomotives off BR, the *50008 'Thunderer'* and *50015 'Valiant'*. Following these purchases, both were moved by rail to the *Longsight Depot* in Manchester, prior to transportation by road to Bury.

The two locomotives made their debut appearance, double-heading a Saturday afternoon service from Bury to Rawtenstall at the ELR's autumn diesel weekend taking place on 3/4 October. Both locomotives were to be looked after by the Manchester Class 50 group. Also appearing at Bury in Autumn 1992 was a rake of six *Mark Two* carriages that were Pete Waterman purchases too.

Meanwhile, in August, it was confirmed that the ELR would be one of only seven railways to host world-famous *LNER A3 Pacific locomotive 'Flying Scotsman'*, now part-owned by Pete Waterman. This was scheduled to take place throughout February 1993 with the train in steam each weekend, alongside additional wine-and-dine services and footplate experiences.

Carriage and Wagon service keeps pace

Since the opening of the line to Rawtenstall, the railway had begun assembling a second rake of coaches. Offering an alternative to the maroon coaches that had operated on the ELR since 1987, this second rake was finished in carmine and cream livery – jokingly referred to as 'blood and custard'. [6]

Also due to make its debut later this year was the *Mark I Second Open carriage M4784* which, with a pronounced similarity to Pullman, was designed to add a more luxurious atmosphere to the rail-track dining experience. The final type of carriage to be brought into service on a safety basis was the *Mark 1 Brake Second Corridor*

(BSK) coach M35314. This would provide a back-up brake coach for the railway should one of the other brake coaches be out of service for any reason.

1993: 'Cracker' all round...

The New Year got off to a great start when ELR's Chief Mechanical Engineer, Ian Riley, sponsored one of the New Year's Day services as '*Riley's Whisky Chaser*', with Ian providing a glass of whisky for any passenger aged over 18 travelling on the train who bought a drink from the on-train buffet. More media involvement came with Pete Waterman's *Class 50 50008 'Thunderer'* being used in an ITV filming of a first episode of '*Cracker*', starring Robbie Coltrane. Filming took place variously on the railway, in the Carriage and Wagon Shed at Buckley Wells and also in the yard of the disused Bury Electric Depot, which had been specially leased from BR for the occasion.

David Flood, a volunteer worker in the Carriage and Wagon department at the time, was later to recall unknowingly becoming involved in a filming shoot: 'We used to work on Tuesday and Thursday evenings in those days. No sooner had I arrived and taken off my coat than C & W Director at the time, Hugh Liney, unexpectedly handed me a crowbar and told me to start jiggling it between the buffers of particular coaches to produce a gentle rocking effect. Adding to the complete mystery for me, the windows of these coaches had been covered in black polythene, leaving me with no idea whatever might be going on inside them.'

Continuing the account: 'It was only later that I came to learn that a scene from the television series '*Cracker*' was being shot. Hugh told me afterwards that he couldn't let on at the time because there was an agreement between the ELR and ITV that all aspects of the production should remain confidential until the episode had appeared on TV.'

The "gentle rocking effect" was to provide a simulated sense of train motion. However, another thing David Flood hadn't been told was that the journey was staged to take place during a rainstorm. He had wondered at the time why there was someone standing on top of the carriage brandishing a hose-pipe. This ended up being aimed down on to the carriage-roof below, conveying the sound of a torrential downpour to those sitting down below inside the covered carriage. All David knew at the time though was that, as well as a sore arm from working on his crowbar, he was also soaked to the skin from the heavy water-spray lashing down on him from above.

Unique history of the *'Flying Scotsman'*

Rescued from the breaker's yard by Alan Pegler in 1962, it seemed remarkable that the iconic engine, *Flying Scotsman,* now in pristine restored condition, should in February 1993 be about to embark on a month-long visit to the ELR.

Since 1962, *Flying Scotsman* had experienced a great number of highs and lows. Following an overhaul on the locomotive in the winter of 1968/9, the adventurous Pegler had received the blessing of then Prime Minister Harold Wilson to take his prize asset across the Atlantic, with the financial backing of the Government, to the USA and Canada on a lengthy tour 'supporting British exports'.

In order to comply with American railway regulations though, '*Scotsman*' had been required to undergo certain transcontinental adaptations, for example needing to be fitted with cowcatcher, bell, buckeye couplings, an American-style whistle, air brakes and high intensity headlamp. However, starting out from Boston, Massachusetts, the enterprise had run into even more serious logistical issues after the engine was classified a fire hazard. The only way round this involved the engine having to be towed by a diesel, adding considerably to running costs.

For the next two years, *Scotsman* embarked on a tour the length and breadth of the North American continent. In the meantime though, a change of government took place in the UK, the sting in the tail being that new Prime Minister Edward Heath had pulled the plug on funding. This meant Pegler having to pick up the expenses tab on his own. By the end of 1972, money had run dry. Pegler was declared bankrupt, in debt to the tune of £132,000. *Scotsman* had to be left in storage at the US Army's Sharpe Depot in Lathrop, California, to keep it out of the way of unpaid creditors. In 1973, during the course of a rescue mission, *Flying Scotsman* was sold off to British rail enthusiast William McAlpine (a member of the wealthy "concrete" family), who put in place arrangements to ship the prized engine back safely to the UK.

Meanwhile, Pegler worked his passage home from San Francisco to England on a P&O cruise ship in 1971, paying his way by giving lectures on the topic of "trains and travel" to passengers. Formally declared bankrupt in the High Court in 1972, he lived thereafter in rented accommodation above a fish and chip shop opposite Paddington Station. Nevertheless, Alan Pegler survived a further forty years, surprisingly earning his crust as an actor, playing the role of Henry VIII over 700 times in productions staged at the *Tower of London*.

Passing away in 2012 at the age of 91, he never forsook his fondness for *Flying Scotsman*. On 13 October 2018, his ashes were taken on board *Scotsman* on a journey from King's Cross to York. As he had wished for, they were scattered in the firebox as the train ascended Stoke Bank between Peterborough and Grantham. His daughter Penny Vaudoyer was on the footplate.

As for the new owner of *Flying Scotsman* from 1973 onwards, Sir William McAlpine (acquiring a knighthood after inheriting the family baronetcy on the death of his father in 1990) had entertained somewhat less ambitious plans for the engine, maintaining and running *'Scotsman'* as a service solely intended for the benefit of the British railway system and rail enthusiasts. McAlpine had paid for its restoration at *Derby Works*. In Summer 1973, the locomotive had been transferred to *Steamtown* in Carnforth, from where it went on regular tours. Over the subsequent 23 years in which McAlpine was to keep ownership, the locomotive underwent two further costly overhauls.

In October 1988, at the invitation of the Australian Government, *Scotsman* featured in the country's bicentenary celebrations. Before long, the locomotive had set yet another record en route from Alice Springs to Melbourne, travelling 679 kilometres (422 miles) from Parkes to Broken Hill non-stop, the longest run by a steam locomotive ever recorded. Despite such an accolade, McAlpine had felt constrained during the course of 1993 to sell *Flying Scotsman* in order to pay off a mortgage on the locomotive, resulting in the end in a merger with Pete Waterman to form '*Flying Scotsman Railways*' with the latter running the business side of the partnership.

Flying Scotsman arrives on ELR track in February 1993

Marking the occasion in style, Piper Frank Warburton heralded the arrival of the *Flying Scotsman* at Bury Bolton Street station at the start of February 1993 with a rendition of '*Scotland the Brave*'.

The legendary engine's visit to the ELR, lasting throughout February, involved four return services at the weekends and also three between 22 and 26 February to coincide with the half-term school holiday. Despite its illustrious past records, the highest speed the '*Scotsman*' was destined to achieve during the course of the month was 20 mph, a speed limitation put in place for practical reasons. The immense weight of the locomotive meant its speed had to be severely restricted on the relatively lightweight, short-distance ELR track it was running on.

However, on a positive note, it gave ELR spectators opportunity to gain more time to view the world-famous flyer in action. On the final weekend, '*Flying Scotsman*' carried a wreath in tribute to 16-year-old Stephen Wright - the son of ELRPS's Chairman - who had died a few days beforehand after a brave fight against leukaemia.

Historic Steam Railway Festival: August 1993

Twenty acres of derelict railway land at Buckley Wells were acquired this year, complete with Grade II-listed carriage shed. In view of the planned integration of the Metrolink and ELR services, it was a strategically important site, being close to the proposed Metrolink park and ride station.

In August 1993, the ELR hosted one of the most ambitious events in railway preservation history to date - a month-long *Steam Railway Festival* to commemorate the 25th anniversary of the end of steam traction on British Railway lines. With respect to its own year of foundation, 1993 also marked the 25th anniversary of the formation of the East Lancashire Railway Preservation Society at Helmshore in 1968.

Throughout the intervening years, the ELR had gone on enhancing its status as a reliable railway to which owners might hire their locomotives. Many strong relationships had been built up between owners and the railway. Ian Riley, in his capacity as Chief Mechanical Engineer, had played a notable part in forging good relations over the years. In 1993, he re-located his locomotive engineering business from Kirkby in Merseyside to Bury.

Leading up to the Festival event, frantic work went on in order to house a wide variety of locomotives in the newly-christened 'ELR Locomotive Works'. A star attraction was *LMS 'Coronation' Pacific 4-6-2 6233 'Duchess of Sutherland'*. The Stanier-designed locomotive was currently owned by *Bressingham Steam Museum*, near Diss in Norfolk. Unfortunately, the combined cost of bringing such a distinguished A-list of locomotives together for all of a month meant that, despite the huge amount of positive publicity and goodwill engendered, the event ran at a financial loss. Despite this, the size and scope of the 1993 event handsomely illustrated the impressive journey the ELR had made during its first 25 years of operation.

At a ceremony held on 8 January 1994, the ELR was presented with the prestigious *Association of Railway Preservation Society Award for 1993* in recognition of the railway's success in bringing together 18 locomotives at the summer *Steam Railway Festival* event. Also that year, Ramsbottom Station Master Brian Almond, together with ELR Publicity Director Graham Vevers and Steven Lever from Bury Council, had attended a ceremony at the *Royal College of Arts* in London to receive an *Ian Allan Heritage Award* in recognition of the transformation of Ramsbottom station.

Bury Bolton Street station is refurbished: 1994

On the site of the long-demolished ELR headquarters building alongside Platform 2, restorative work took place during 1994, including the construction of a new café building, to be named *'Trackside'*. Since the re-opening of the line in 1987, the ELR had relied on a *Mark* 1 Restaurant coach for catering at the station, with the additional seating provision of a Mark 1 TSO coach on Platform 4. The new *'Trackside'* featured a large dining area with capacity for

80 diners, a kitchen area, store rooms and toilet facilities. The café opened in December 1994, just in time to offer valuable back-up provision for *Santa Specials*.

More work was carried out at the station during 1995 - courtesy of a '*Derelict Grant Fund*' award - on strengthening the bridge carrying Bolton Street over the railway, alongside the station building. At the same time, the lay-by in front of the station was removed with the street re-modelled to widen scope for passing road traffic.

A project to refurbish the station as a whole had to be undertaken because of damage from water ingress through the roof. This did not begin until the end of 1995 and continued into 1996. After work on waterproofing, the shop, information office, booking office, booking hall and staircases were re-plastered and re-wired. A disabled access lift was installed on the staircase leading down to Platforms 3/4. As in the case of the recently refurbished Rawtenstall station, a key feature at Bolton Street was the clock tower at the entrance to the station.

Lions on the right tracks: 1995

In May 1995, 'the first railway carriage in the country uniquely designed for disabled rail travellers had been launched on the ELR'. Up to this point, disabled people journeying on the Bury to Rawtenstall line had had to travel in the guard's van, separated from relatives and friends. From now on though, due to the active work put in by former ELR member Albert Potter together with very gratefully-received financial support from *Peel Lions*, (the Ramsbottom-based charity organisation originally set up in 1974) disabled passengers were able to travel in a purpose-built facility. This new provision came with specially widened doors and electrically-operated ramps, a disabled toilet as well as a buffet and PA system. It had capacity to carry up to 18 wheelchairs with 10 seats for other passengers, including helpers. [7]

Pete Waterman's entrepreneurial role extended

As a member of the *Stock, Aitken and Waterman* song-writing team, Pete Waterman had first made his name and fortune in the music industry, writing and producing many hit singles. Having started his working life as a steam fireman though, he had also by now come to be well-known for his enthusiasm for railways. Pete's association with the ELR had begun in 1988 with the purchase of his first diesel locomotive, *25909.* As his collection grew, he had established a base at *Crewe Heritage Centre*, reviving the name of the London & North Western Railway in a new company called LNWR Heritage which undertook restoration of locomotives purchased by Waterman.

In support of the 1995 ELR *Diesel Event*, Waterman Railways once again supplied a convoy of visiting locomotives from Crewe. In 1996 however, much of the Waterman Railways collection of locomotives and coaches was to be sold off, following Pete's decision to move away from running charter services on the national network. He was though to remain heavily supportive of the ELR in future years. For example, *1501 Gateshead* and his *GWR Observation Saloon* were kept on at the ELR after the selling-off of much of the rest of his collection. He also continued to supply locomotives for ELR events and was later made President of the ELRPS in recognition of his longstanding support for the railway.

Tributes paid to three ELR stalwarts: 1996

Tributes were paid during the course of 1996 to three ELR members who each, in their own distinctive way, had made highly significant contributions to the development of the organisation from its earliest days onwards.

Geoff Parkington, the former ELRPS Membership Secretary and Stations Administration Manager passed away on 17 July. Geoff had been responsible for the setting up of booking office procedures when the railway first re-opened in 1987 and been a regular booking clerk at Bury Bolton Street station until standing down from those duties in 1995. His anecdotes for the ELR News Magazines, entitled '*Babbling from the Booking Office*', had regularly provided a humorous, "chestnuts" feature for readers, as for example – Passenger: "Can I take my dog on the train?" Booking clerk: "So long as he doesn't bite the guard".

Joe Strickleton was a longstanding steam department volunteer and one of the most highly regarded members of the footplate crews. He had been honoured by being chosen to drive *ELR 'No. 1'* on the historic occasion of the re-opening of the Bury-Rawtenstall line on 27 April 1991. In the early hours of 28 September, Joe had passed away in his sleep. He had been on company business the evening before, driving *45337* on a dining service.

News had also come of the death of Walter Baker on 20 October in this same year, 1996. Walter had been highly influential in the formation of the original Helmshore and District Railway Preservation Society back in 1966, later in 1968 becoming the first Chairman of the ELRPS. Although not an active member in more recent times, due to illness, his earlier contribution to the cause of the Society was strongly acknowledged by all those who followed in his footsteps. Harry Hatcher wrote: 'I express the condolences to his family and those of "The Few" that remain from the early days of the Society, who will no doubt, like myself, have a lasting affectionate memory of Walter, typically with a cigarette hanging from the corner of his mouth and having a good cough, shouldering the woes of the society and getting on with the job'. [8]

150-year celebrations honour opening of ELR line: 1996

Celebrating the opening of the original East Lancashire Railway line, which had taken place on 28 September 1846, a number of events were organised throughout August and September 1996, with a VIP celebration taking place on 25 September. The occasion started with speeches and presentations on Platform 2 at Bury Bolton Street. ELRPS Chairman Harry Hatcher welcomed guests and then invited the Lord Lieutenant of Greater Manchester, Colonel John Timmins, to unveil a plaque on the wall of the new café building on Platform 2.

At 13.15, the Mayor of Bury, Trevor Holt, waved a green flag and blew a guard's whistle. A conspicuous presence on the day was ELRPS Membership Secretary and Guard David Flood who, in accordance with 1840s fashion, had acquired bushy sideburns and moustache for the occasion. Locomotives ex-L&Y *A class 0-6-0 1300* disguised as ELR locomotive '*150*' and Paddy Smith's *Black 5 No. 5407* double-headed the special train which had come from Buckley Wells.

The other main highlight on the day had been the formal handover at 12.45 of the National Railway Museum's *Hughes-Fowler 'Crab'*

2700, the occasion being serenaded by the *Brass Band* from *Burnley Towneley High School*. The locomotive, which had spent a number of years assigned to Bury steam shed, had been placed on loan to the ELR. *2700* was handed over by the NRM's Head of Operations Ray Towell and a short ceremony took place on Platform 4 at Bury Bolton Street, with ELR Chairman Trevor Jones accepting the immaculate LMS lined-black liveried locomotive from the NRM.

The train departed at 1.30 pm and was paused on arrival at Ramsbottom so that travelling guests had chance both to visit the town and engage in conversation with a number of civic leaders and local business people. This was before moving on to Rawtenstall, where another plaque was unveiled, with ELRPS President Les Ratcliffe officiating. Guests were invited to partake of a buffet lunch, served on board the ELR's dedicated dining coaches that had been stabled in the bay platform at Rawtenstall earlier in the day.

Stepping up ELR business promotion

Given the rapid pace at which the company's business was expanding, the ELR Board of Directors decided it was necessary to appoint a full-time salaried General Manager to co-ordinate day-to-day management. Long-term volunteer Tim Hanson was chosen for the post which was in the first instance couched as 'General Manager Designate'. Tim had joined the Society in 1978. In 1981, he had purchased *D1041 'Western Prince'* and brought it to Bury. Two years later, he had also acquired *'Hymek' No. D7076*. More recently, he had joined with Ian Riley, Richard Law and Roy Syrett in purchasing ex-GWR *2-8-2T No. 7229* for restoration.

Starting out in the new role on 6 January 1997, Tim's main responsibility was to promote the use of the railway during the quieter midweek periods when the ELR was not running timetabled passenger services. As an example of an ever-growing number of media-based projects conducted on the ELR line, filming for the BBC drama, *'Hetty Wainthrop Investigates'* took place in 1997. Featuring Patricia Routledge in the eponymous role, the ELR line lay at the heart of a number of scenes in the programme, mainly set around Irwell Vale and Rawtenstall. The locomotive *Stanier 5MT 4-6-0, 5407* played a notable part in proceedings.

Following its starring role in '*Hetty Wainthrop*', *5407* was withdrawn from service to allow its compulsory ten-yearly service to be carried out. It also marked a change of ownership for the locomotive with Ian Riley purchasing the popular '*Black Five*' from Paddy Smith. Ian immediately set about an overhaul, with the aim of having it back in service by summer 1998.

£1.1million funding package is secured for the '***Heywood Link***'

Almost miraculously, funding amounting to £1,128,000 came through in 1998 in the form of substantial grant contributions from *English Partnerships*, Bury, Rossendale and Rochdale Councils, along with waste management company, *Pilsworth Environmental.*

The funding was intended to enable several major projects to be carried out, including:

- The construction of a new platform at Heywood station
- The extension of the platform at Rawtenstall station to accommodate nine-coach trains
- The installation of a major signalling scheme at Bury Bolton Street, involving the full re-commissioning of Bury South signal box
- Major track alterations at Bury Bolton Street, including the re-connection of the north end of Platform 4 to service through trains, as well as Platforms 2 and 3
- Refurbishment of Roch Viaduct which would involve replacing the deck and waterproofing.

To celebrate the award of this grant funding, a special '*Heywood Link 2000*' train was operated on 28 October 1998, with *45407* and *Class 47, 1501*, topping and tailing the train which had been given dispensation to run by the Railway Inspectorate. Soon after, contractors began on the refurbishment of Roch Viaduct, with the track being lifted by the end of October. The grant awarding marked a most positive step forward, although it was recognised it would still take a lot more work before the Heywood line would be fit to re-open for running regular passenger services.

Moving towards the new Millennium

In May 1999, a filming contract with Channel 4 television revolved around reconstructing the *Great Train Robbery* of 1963 for a documentary programme. The film company had wanted to use the ELR-based *Class 40 D335* owing to the fact it was identical to the locomotive involved in the infamous robbery. However, because *D335* happened to be out of service undergoing repairs, the locomotive and three vans were in the final outcome propelled along the line by *D345*.

During the same month, on Wednesday 19 May, the York *National Railway Museum*-owned replica of George Stephenson's '*Rocket*', driven by the *NRM*'s Ray Towell, hauled two period coaches over the "soon to be re-opened" four-mile stretch of ELR extension line between Bury and Heywood. The locomotive had just completed a three-week stay at the railway, where it had been engaged in the filming of a production for '*Wind Fall Films*' set during the time of the Industrial Revolution.

Meanwhile, during the 1999 May Bank Holiday weekend, the ELR line was transformed back in time to the 1940s with the holding of the first '*Railway at War Weekend*' event. Organised by Stations Administration Manager, Neil Parkington, one of Geoff's two sons, the event succeeded in staging a series of re-enactments and parades, as well as witnessing many attendees evoking the spirit of the war-time period by donning 1940s outfits and uniform to honour the occasion. All in all, a befitting way to see out the 20th century and bring in the new Millennium.

Notes

1. Summer/Autumn 1990 *ELR News Magazine*, p.6 2
2. Winter/Spring 1991 *ELR News Magazine*, p.26
3. As for Item above, p.32
4. Andrew Coward, *East Lancashire Railway*, p.41
5. David Mather, *East Lancashire Railway Recollection*, (2015) Silver Link Publishing Ltd. p.7
6. Andrew Coward, *East Lancashire Railway Back In Time: 1987-1999*, p.94

7. *Bury Times,* 5 May 1995
8. Winter/Spring 1997 *ELR News Magazine*, p.12

City of Truro at Heywood-Station

Corrie wedding mayhem

John Ellis, Chairman National Railway Heritage Awards- Mike Ashworth, Design and Heritage Manager London Underground- Mrs Lois Vevers and Peter Duncan, Chairman of the East Lancashire Railway. May 2012

Opening of Burrs Park train stop 2016

Linda Henderson- first ever female mainline locomotive driver with proud mum Margaret Wilson at her side.

City of Wells poster

Pete Waterman appeal during Covid

Long Service Awards

Black Horse advert

Union of South Africa

Father Christmas (aka Pete Beetham) and Elf (aka wife Sheila) on the Santa Special

City of Wells

Crossing Brooksbottom

Flying Scotsman

Michael Portillo visits the ELR June 2023.Second left Mike Kelly and right Richard Law.

Sir Nigel Gresley

Chapter Ten – Heading out to Heywood

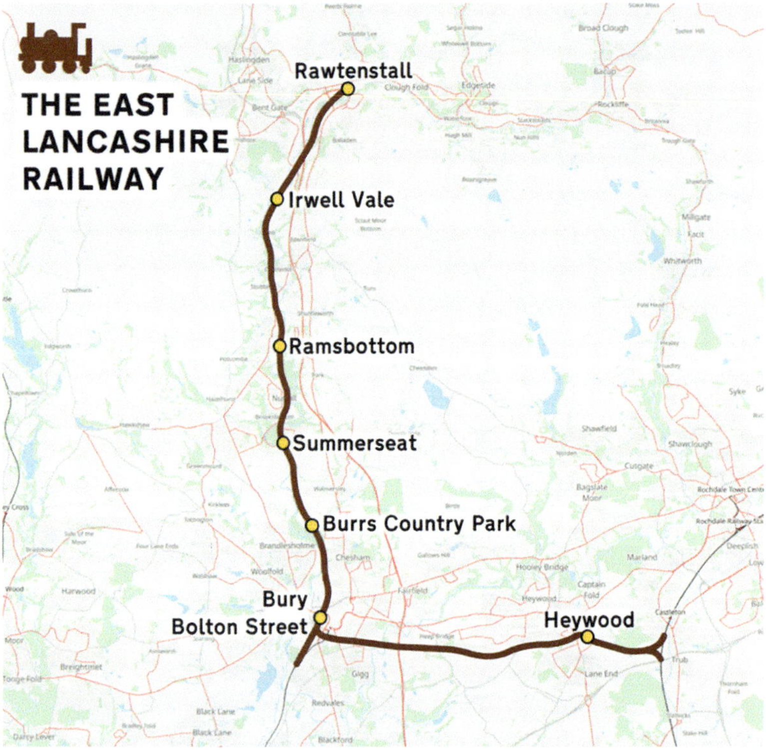

The ELR in modern times

Peter Duncan becomes Chairman of the ELR Light Railway Company

Justifiable tribute was paid to Trevor Jones upon his standing down as Chairman in 2000. A founder member on the ELRPS Council from 1969 before becoming Chair of the ELR Light Railway Company in 1970, Trevor had played a pre-eminent part in the opening of the

Bury to Ramsbottom line in 1987 and extension to Rawtenstall in 1991.

Trevor was succeeded by Peter Duncan, with a work background centring on the British Rail Manchester Area Civil Engineers Office. Phil Bailey, who had been an ELR volunteer since the very early days, worked in the same office. Later to take on the role of Director of Civil Engineering himself, Phil had encouraged Peter to enlist as an ELR volunteer.

Peter's first major role had been as Road Vehicles Officer for the ELR's Bury Transport Museum. As the prospect of re-opening the railway to Ramsbottom began to open up more, Peter had subsequently become ELR Signalling Director. The formation of a small Signal Engineering Department quickly followed, leading to important work being carried out at Bury and Ramsbottom before the re-opening of the line in 1987.

Next milestone had been to Rawtenstall in 1991 which required the re-signalling of Ramsbottom station, along with restoration of the level crossings at Townsend Fold and Rawtenstall West. From 1999 onwards, Peter had played a leading part in the task of re-signalling in and around Bury Bolton Street station.

Heywood to Rawtenstall- Gradient Profile

Completing the Rail Link from Bury to Heywood: 2003

Up to the start of 2001, much of the on-going work to open the ELR's connecting line to Heywood involved remodelling the track-work at Bury South junction in order to allow trains onto the Heywood line;

also to control the passage of locomotives and trains from the carriage sidings and the locomotive works.

Meanwhile, work at the other end of the line included reinstating the platform at Heywood station and providing a run-round loop for locomotives. What was now the third reincarnation of Heywood station (the one before having closed on 5 October 1970) was opened in September 2003. It was located slightly further to the east of the second station, nearer to the former Heywood railway wagon works. A 'jack leg' cabin was to serve as a booking office and waiting room. The car park at Heywood station occupies the site of the former wagon goods yard and has made use of the original setts which provided access between the first sidings, offering a distinctive arrival-area for modern day travellers to the station.

Whilst there is no doubt that Trevor Jones' networking and negotiating skills had played a significant part in the early years of ELR life, the benefits arising from Peter Duncan's strong railway background came in most useful when plans to open up to Heywood required practical application.

The line extension had to cross over the Manchester Metrolink to Bury, at the site of the former Bury Knowsley Street station. This necessitated the construction of a new intersection bridge, with steeply graded approaches reaching maxima of 1 in 36 and 1 in 41 nicknamed '*The Ski Jump*'. There was also need for a replacement bridge at Pilsworth Road. The opening date when the ELR would start to operate a service of regular passenger trains to Heywood was finalised for Saturday 6 September 2003.

With the *Whitworth Vale Band* providing a rousing send-off, '*Leander*' conveyed the 300 passengers, travelling in six carriages, away from Rawtenstall station at 11 o'clock in the morning. Despite rainy weather, the celebratory journey to Heywood took place amidst great excitement.

Heading towards Bury, the train rose majestically over the top of the M66 – the only preserved railway in the country to surmount a motorway. However, things did not go exactly to plan on the day. 'The train had been negotiating a particularly steep curve about 200 yards from the platform at Bury Bolton Street when the beautiful burgundy 70 feet long *'Leander'* skipped off the rails, leaving her tender still on the tracks but her engine off them. The engine was quickly uncoupled and left on the tracks while the diesel, somewhat less ceremonially, hauled the six coaches back to Rawtenstall.' [1]

Maintaining the spirit of the day though, passengers arriving at Heywood were welcomed by the *Heywood and Middleton Brass Band* and due ceremony unfolded. The stretch of line was officially opened by Pete Waterman, together with Mayor of Rochdale, Councillor Sultan Ali.

The ELR Heritage line now ran to just over 12 miles (19k) and potentially had a mainline connection with the national railway network at Castleton, the boundary between the two lines a short distance east of the station at Hopwood, beyond which the regulatory body was Railtrack, later to be succeeded by Network Rail. Despite the transfer of the Manchester-Bury line from BR to Metrolink having appeared to mean the loss of the ELR's direct link to the national network, the company still held out hope of retrieving linkage.

'Brief Encounter'

In February 2004, the *East Lancs Pioneer* train travelled from London King's Cross to Rawtenstall, the first passenger train to come to the Valley from the national network for more than thirty years, something that Trevor Jones had dreamt about happening again one day. The stop at Rawtenstall was described in the press as a 'brief encounter' because there ended up being only five minutes for passengers to take in some fresh air on the platform before the train had to hare back down on the return trip south. It had been intended to stop longer but due to unforeseen delays along the way, time needed to be made up on the schedule. [2]

Even so, the journey had proved a memorable one. Passengers in the sixteen heritage carriages had been driven by electric train from King's Cross to Doncaster before changing to a diesel locomotive and then cutting cross-country through Huddersfield to Heywood and from there on to Rawtenstall. The running of this tour provided the latest milestone in the ELR's list of achievements, coming only a few months after the re-opening of the line to Heywood.

1940s '*Wartime Weekends*' - 2005 onwards

2005 marked the 60th anniversary of both VE and VJ days with a bumper programme of commemorative events, probably the most notable being a *Battle of Britain* fly-past of vintage planes.

2008 proved a special year marking the:

1. 40th Anniversary of the last steam train operated by British Railway.
2. 10th year of the running of ELR's *Wartime Weekend.*
3. 40th Anniversary of the ELRPS.

There was no doubting the continued popularity of this annual occasion which succeeded in attracting thousands of visitors over the three days it ran, including two evening dances. The ELR (with Neil Parkington continuing to act as chief co-ordinator) had become one of the leading, national exponents of this type of event with visitors flocking here from all parts of the country. A large number were 're-enactors', adopting the wartime spirit and dress of the 1940s. 3

Tributes paid to Trevor Jones

Following a short illness, aged 61, Trevor Jones died on 30 November 2006 at *Springhill Hospice.* His lifetime contribution to the ELR had been immense.

Amongst the many tributes paid, Harry Hatcher recalled having 'attended many meetings with Trevor, both as Chairman of the Society and a member of the ELR Railway Trust. His confident statements of what we could undertake and achieve often influenced the decisions and made the difference between success and failure'. 4

With a flair for acquiring assets for the company, Trevor was highly resourceful in procuring a great number of industrial locomotives and rolling stock items. The main driving force behind the opening of the ELR heritage line between Bury and Ramsbottom in 1987, followed by extension of the route to Rawtenstall in 1991, Trevor had stepped down from the role of Chairman in 2000 even though remaining a company director.

The last official duty he performed was to meet a Chinese delegation at Ramsbottom station in May 2006 and, despite being seriously ill at this point in time, he had been organising a mayoral visit to the railway in 2007. This same year coincided with the 20th anniversary of the re-opening of the Bury to Ramsbottom line in which special honour was bestowed on Trevor with the *40145 East Lancashire Railway* named after him – *Trevor Jones'*.

20th Anniversary of the Re-opening of the Bury-Ramsbottom Line - 2007

A celebration lasting five days took place (25–29 July 2007) to mark 20 years since the line re-opening. On Wednesday 25 July, a re-enactment train (11.05 departure), double-headed by *0-6-0ST's No. 70* (Manchester Ship Canal) and *No. 140* (National Coal Board) conveyed guests travelling in six carriages from Bolton Bury Street to Ramsbottom. A reception was held at the station with music played by the *Westwood Over-55s Brass Band*. A plaque was unveiled to mark the occasion before the train returned to Bury, followed by a reception in the *Elizabethan Suite* at Bury Town Hall.

During the rest of the day, and throughout Thursday 26 and Friday 27, in accordance with the 1987 timetable, the railway continued to operate a shuttle passenger service between Heywood and Bury. It was hauled by guest loco *3440 'City of Truro'* and from Bury to Ramsbottom using the two *0-6-0ST* tank locomotives and coaching stock. From Ramsbottom to Rawtenstall, a *DMU* service was in operation.

Over the weekend of 28/29 July, Ramsbottom station played host to a miniature railway for children's rides with other attractions on offer to visitors, including *Disco Dancing Demonstration, Funfair and Morris Dancing*. At Bury station, visitors had the chance to enjoy a '*Standard Gauge Locomotive Driving Experience*' as well as there being Bury Transport Museum vehicles on display and a '*Thomas Event*' demonstration.

New General Manager with a passion for railway preservation

Andy Coward, General Manager since February, introduced himself to ELR members as follows: 'Some of you may recognise my name as

I used to regularly contribute to the ELR News and up until moving to Nottingham in 2002, I was a regular volunteer on the railway for many years, where I undertook a wide variety of roles and it was the ELR where I first discovered my passion for railway preservation'. 5

Back in 1998, Andy had served as Assistant General Manager for twelve months before leaving for a job in the light rail (tramway) industry spending three years at Manchester Metrolink where he worked as an Inspector and Driver. Before returning to ELR, his five-year long job in Nottingham had involved setting up the Nottingham Express Transit tramway. What he described as a brief but highly enjoyable period working as a writer for *Rail Magazine* had followed before taking up his new position back with the ELR.

Metrolink and the part played by ELR in its refurbishment

In January 2006, the *Greater Manchester Passenger Transport Executive (GMPTE)* had first approached the ELR with a proposal to utilise its connection with Network Rail at Hopwood Junction to enable all the materials needed for the Bury line renewal to be brought in by rail over ELR metals. A plan emerged to the effect that haulage of materials should be carried out by a freight operating company. This would entail the use of an amount of spare ground, adjacent to the ELR locomotive works at Baron Street, for the stockpiling of materials.

Having invited tenders, *GMPTE* awarded the contract to *Carillion Rail* from the three received. ELR was involved at each stage of the process with Chairman Peter Duncan fortunate to call on the negotiating skills and experience of Malcolm Vickers acting as Project Director. An important condition agreed upon was that all the additional track-work and connections made were to remain ELR property after completion of the project.

The Baron Street site needed sifting in order to identify items worth preserving. These were found new homes elsewhere on the railway, the remainder scrapped. In May 2007, several excavators and bulldozers were brought in to clear the site and prepare the surface for subsequent tracklaying, materials storage and temporary office accommodation.

Six ELR staff were selected to carry out the schedule of work: Malcolm Frost, Frank Cronin, Brian Topping, Brian Sutcliffe, Roland Hatton and Richard Law. Signalmen were required to work Bury South box with Phil Baguley, Charlie Tallis, Roger Healey and Rob Newton offering their services. Another specialised group of staff provided by ELR were the shunter-guards. The whole operation required a strong degree of co-ordination by Operations Duty Supervisor Richard Law, with the assistance of John Yates, Phil Gater and John Hobbs. For legal and health and safety reasons, all these personnel were awarded fixed term contracts of employment with East Lancashire Light Railway Co. Ltd.

During the period of the contract, added complications arose from the fact that the ELR had to go on carrying out its midweek service between Bolton Street and Rawtenstall. An excellent safety record was maintained throughout. In terms of acquired infrastructure, the ELR benefitted from two new sidings, others being re-ballasted, eleven lighting towers, the whole site being cleared of accumulated 'lost causes' together with tons of scrub. Meanwhile, the outcome of the operation had provided various areas of hardstanding as well as several internal access roads being improved upon.

ELR's involvement in this project served to illustrate that, although not a company consisting of full-time paid railway staff, its team had proved highly competent and successful from both operational and commercial standpoints.

'*Santa Specials* - Thank you to the assorted cast!'

The 2008 *Santa Specials* proved an outstanding success with the revenue accrued achieving record new profits. It was noted that: 'this event is by far the largest profit provider in the Railway's year. To put things into perspective, the profit it generates exceeds that of all other special events put together. During the eleven opening days, nearly 25,000 passengers were carried.'

Gratitude towards the involvement of ELR staff was underlined in the following statement made by Bob Johnson: 'On behalf of the Chairman and Board, I would like to thank all those who took part in the 2008 *Santa* operation, midweek volunteers, retail shop staff, booking and information office staff, present pickers, sherry and mince pie team, station staff, buffet and trolley staff, badge staff, *Santas*, fairies and elves, train managers and stewards, drivers, firemen, second men, guards, C + W staff, ROs, signalmen, carriage cleaners, TTIs (Travelling Ticket Inspectors) etc, for a job very well done.' [6]

Les Ratcliffe MBE

On the sad news of the death of Les Ratcliffe on 12 June 2009, Harry Hatcher wrote in tribute that after the ELRPS had been first formed in 1968, there hadn't been thought anyone fit to serve in the role of President. 'However, all that changed by 1981 when the name of Les Ratcliffe had come forward.

'A well-respected and prominent local businessman, Les was duly elected as the ELR's first President. He was always ready to help where he could and for example he and his wife Nancy would be at Bolton Street, or wherever we were holding an event, providing a buffet for the members attending'.

After the railway re-opened in 1987, a number of Diner Trains were chartered in aid of Bury Hospice, another interest of Les. 'By the time he decided to step down as President in 2007, Harry Hatcher remarked, 'he was Les Ratcliffe MBE, an honour richly deserved for his services to the community'. [7]

ELRPS Membership reaches new high

By March 2009, ELRPS membership had soared to an all-time high, standing at 4,150 – which was 129 higher than at the same time the year before. Many members also took advantage of new membership schemes that were introduced this year, for example 3-year and Senior Life Membership.

Halloween Ghost Train

A new special event for 2009 (operating on 31 October) was the *Halloween Ghost Train*, providing free travel for children in scary outfits, with accompanying adults charged £10 for the return journey between Bury and Rawtenstall. The event caught the public imagination to the extent that queues stretched all the way down Bolton Street and the railway had to put on a second train to satisfy demand.

Brand new start for the Bury Transport Museum

On 26 March 2010, HRH the Duke of Gloucester arrived by train from Heywood to open the re-furbished Bury Transport Museum at Castlecroft. Work had been on-going for the last three years costing a total of £3 million. Malcolm Vickers had carried overall responsibility for the project. Assistance (manual and financial) was forthcoming from the Society with Andy Hardman playing a prominent part in proceedings. The aim was to celebrate the history of transport while at the same time using brighter and more advanced technology to bring it to life in a way that appealed to younger visitors.

As well as the vintage vehicles, there were various hands-on models showing for example how bridges, engines and levers worked. Increased use of the facilities came through waves of school parties visiting. In the first year, 75 different schools visited, making up a total of approximately 3,000 pupils. The most popular activity was the *'Evacuees Experience'*, for which pupils went on a train-ride, clutching name-label and gas mask.

It was the first time that many had seen a steam engine, let alone travelled on one. Corridor coaches with compartments were used to relate further to the kind of train-ride evacuees would have experienced – in line with *'Harry Potter'!*

Coronation Street 'wedding event'

Filming took place at the ELR in June and July 2010 of a particularly dramatic episode of *'Coronation Street'*. Characters Hayley and Roy Cropper (played respectively by Accrington-born Julie Hesmondhalgh and David Neilson) were travelling with guests to their wedding event aboard an ELR train of *Mark* 1 coaches, hauled by LMS *'Black 5' No. 44871*, bearing *45407's Lancashire Fusilier* nameplates for the occasion.

The storyline put a spanner in the works however! Florist Mary Taylor, jealous for some reason, had engineered the uncoupling of the rear coach containing the bridal party. A frantic scene ensued involving bride Hayley, resplendent in wedding dress, having no alternative but to clamber on to an air pump trolley in an attempt to re-connect to the main body of the train. Meanwhile bridesmaids Becky and Fiz, also dressed up-to-the-nine, strutted their stuff having to pump the trolley handle up and down for all they were worth to make up the ground. The episode was transmitted to ITV viewers on August Bank Holiday.

Hollyoaks 'fireball'

ELR also 'starred' in the BBC television film '*Eric and Ernie*', shown on New Year's Day 2011, which was about the early career of the British comedy duo Morecambe and Wise. Bury Bolton Street station was featured, along with a train of *Mark 1* coaches hauled by *LMS 'Black 5' No. 44871.*

The longest commitment to filming on ELR lines was to be made by *Channel Four* in the course of a 13-day *Hollyoaks* shoot in 2014. Featuring another wedding scene, this one was destined though to make the plight of Corrie's nuptial occasion look tame by comparison, involving the derailing of a train with one of the wedding party coaches being blown up in a huge fireball.

Age Profile of ELR Membership

A graph was presented in 2011 showing the age profile of membership. Not surprisingly, the highest number of members by far fell within the 60 to 70 year-old bracket.

Exploring underlying reasons why this should be so, *ELR Magazine* Editor David Flood posed the question: 'Is this because 60 to 70 year-olds can remember steam as it was? Being 60 years of age means that when steam disappeared in this area, we were 17 years of age...What are we looking at here? A large group of individuals aged 60 to 70 who will diminish with time and have no replacements or is this simply the way things are, and will remain, with a high retired age profile?' [8]

The issues posed were indeed relevant in terms of projecting membership numbers in future years. Not least, it was accepted that more needed to be done to engage younger age-groups to join.

Tributes to Graham Vevers

Graham Vevers, a long-serving and highly-respected ELR stalwart, passed away on 9 April 2012, aged 69. Graham had first become involved with the railway restoration project in his mid-20s. He had gone to Helmshore to find out what was happening with regard to the proposed closure of the station. After attending the 1971 ELPRS AGM, he arrived home to inform his wife Lois that he had been elected to the post of Treasurer. In many ways, the path Graham was to follow reflected the tenacious and adaptable character of the ELR as it subsequently developed.

Forty years later, at the 2011 AGM, he was warmly congratulated on his outstanding service over a sustained period of time, being by far the longest serving officer in the history of the Society. Much had changed in financial terms in the meantime. For example, when the company had first started, about 80% of its income was generated from enthusiasts with only 20% deriving from what might loosely be called tourism enterprises. '*Thomas the Tank Engine*' and '*Santa Specials*' were in large measure responsible for the swing in revenue-source.

Graham had taken on other duties over the years, including that of Stations Director. In 1989, he had joined the ELLR.Co Board as Marketing Director, submitting many applications for awards, many of which were successful. He worked tirelessly in supporting the Chairman of the ELR, Trevor Jones up to 2001 and subsequently Peter Duncan.

Chairman & Signalling Director Peter Duncan paid tribute to Graham, saying that 'he was a very quiet and private individual, who got on with all these things without fuss. I doubt many people had any real knowledge of the full extent of his activities, ably supported by his wife Lois, who was also involved in so much of what Graham did for the ELR'. 9

Restoration of '*Gothenburg*'

During 2013, the ELRPS committed £38,500 in funding to restore *Gothenburg*, the largest single contribution it had donated to the Railway to that point. The engine, built in 1903, had been brought to the ELR after several decades of service on the Manchester Ship Canal. The original intention had been to carry out necessary repair work to get the *Gothenburg* back into steam for the remaining four years of its 'boiler-ticket'. However, on inspection, the opportunity was taken to carry out a full refurbishment so that it would then be enabled to acquire a full 10-year certificate.

Having served the ELR notably well in a variety of ways in past years, featuring for example two celebratory runs commemorating the re-openings from Bury to Ramsbottom in 1987 and from Bury to Rawtenstall in 1991, the engine's 'stardom' became further assured in relation to an on-going spell as '*Thomas the Tank Engine*'.

Plans to link Castleton Station to the ELR

In September 2014, plans to link the heritage line with Castleton were revealed by Mark Robinson, Rochdale Council's planning chief as part of a major regeneration project. The update, presented to Rochdale Township Committee, made reference to ELR's 'master plan' to transform Castleton into its new terminus and create an interchange with the main Calder Valley line. Mr. Robinson mentioned that the authority is looking to install a temporary platform at Castleton station to 'kick-start' the project.

It was appreciated that a permanent platform would eventually be required but 'delivering a short-term facility at relatively modest cost would not only give the ELR a presence in Castleton but also inject a great deal of impetus into the project and provide real and visible evidence to Rochdale residents that the ELR is also their railway.' [10]

New ELRPS Chairman – David Wright

Becoming Chairman of the ELRPS in 2013, David Wright had first joined the Society in 1989. He came from a railway family with his father having worked as a guard based at London Victoria. While working in the Armed Services, he had happened to visit Ramsbottom one day in 1988 and ended up joining the ELR. The first qualification he had gained was as a railway Guard (December 1997). After that, he had become a Responsible Officer from November 2000 onwards and then a Signalman at Ramsbottom from August 2011 onwards.

David had put in a stint as Assistant to the General Manager and also served as Company Secretary for four years. In relation to the commercial side, he had performed as '*Sir Topham Hatt*' at Thomas the Tank engine events in the early 00s and 'donned a red suit to amuse the young travellers on the *Santa Specials*'. [11]

David's spell as Chairman was to last through much of the 2010s, during which time he was involved in significant changes of direction for the company, as described later on in this chapter.

'*Not a job for a woman?*'

The above question was posed by Linda Henderson in the January 2015 *News Magazine* as the title for a thought-provoking article examining the role of women working on the railways over the years. Her trawl through history started at the time of World War I when thousands of male railway employees had been enlisted into the forces, leaving gaps in the workforce needing to be filled by women. For the first two years of the war, this had been seen as a mere stopgap measure. However, the longer the war had carried on, the more evident it had become that women were more than capable of carrying out skilled jobs rather than the stereotypical clerical, catering and cleaning roles traditionally undertaken.

Linda's well-researched article showed that 'our very own L&YR company had employed just over 1,000 women prior to World War I but that by November 1918 were employing over 3,300 women in so-called "male grade" jobs which they performed very ably. However, regrettably, soon after the end of war, the situation had quickly reverted back to women once again consigned to carrying out only the lowest-paid, low-grade roles on the railway'.

A much similar scenario had unfolded in World War II. 'Only it wasn't to prove as easy for the authorities to quash women's aspirations afterwards as easily as it had been after 1918. Following years of wrangling on the matter, a pivotally important realisation of female employment rights came at the start of 1975 with the passing of the *Sex Discrimination Act* which made it illegal to refuse to consider women for roles that had previously been considered to be the sole prerogative of men to apply for'.

In terms of updating to the present day and at the same time contextualising the current role of women within the ELR, Linda continued: 'Here at the ELR, we do have ladies who work for example in clerical and catering roles on the railway but we also have several employed in what might be called more operational roles.

'The jobs that are presently being carried out by women volunteers on the ELR include Driver, Footplate Crew, Guard, Signalman, Ticket Collector as well as the holding of responsibility at the highest level for the running of railway stations. For example, Margaret Wilson has over 21 years' experience as a member of station staff and in excess of 15 years as Station Master at Bury Bolton Street.'

'And me?' Linda continued... 'Well, I've been a volunteer for over 21 years too. I started volunteering during the August festival of steam in 1993...my first duties were as part of station staff, and then as Travelling Ticket Inspector...I'm currently the only female Secondman and Diesel Shunter Driver on the line, and have been a Signalman since I turned 18. I am now also the Signal Operations Department Manager'.

Encouraging more women to come and work for the ELR, Linda had signed off her article: 'We may not be the only ladies working in preservation, but why not come and join us to ensure that we aren't the last?' [12]

By way of on-going evidence of Linda Henderson's own commitment, on 19 March 2017, she was set to become the ELR's first ever mainline driver.

'*Flying Scotsman*' back on ELR lines after £4.2 million restoration

In early 2016, the phenomenon of the *Flying Scotsman* once again bounced back on to ELR lines. On 8 January 2016, the locomotive moved under its own steam for the first time since 2005. The personal journey undergone had been another long and expensive one!

Since February 1993, when the *Scotsman* had put in a month's tour on the ELR, it had then had to endure another overhaul. By 1996, the McAlpine/Waterman partnership had run into financial issues. To help pay off an overdraft, McAlpine had decided to put

Flying Scotsman up for sale. In February 1996, it had been bought by businessman Tony Marchington, already well known in the steam preservation movement, who ran it on mainline tours. However, due to mounting maintenance costs, Marchington was declared bankrupt in September 2003 and forced to sell. Awe-inspiring in so many ways, '*Scotsman*' has never been an easy ride for those taking financial responsibility for it.

Amid fears that the great steam engine might be sold to investors from abroad, the *National Railway Museum* (NRM) in York announced it was launching a bid. Appealing for funds, £415,000 was given by the broader public - together with a donation of £365,000 from entrepreneur Richard Branson as well as a further amount of £1.8m via a grant from the *National Heritage Memorial Fund*. Thus able to remain home-owned, *Scotsman* had arrived in York in time to be on exhibition as part of the museum's '*Railfest*' in June 2004, celebrating 200 years of rail travel.

However, from 2006 onwards, a decade-long restoration project had to be embarked on, costing £4.2 m. Although the Museum's management of the protracted overhaul was heavily criticised in an internally commissioned report in 2012, work was eventually completed. In January 2016, visitors to ELR lines were able to witness first-hand the re-appearance on track of the majestic green and black locomotive. By this point in time, it had been officially credited as "no. 1 best-known train engine" in the history of railways. The accolade had come its way following a worldwide survey conducted by *YouGov* the year before, *Flying Scotsman* topping the poll by a clear margin.

The ELR played a significant part in the *Scotsman's* resurgence, with the honour bestowed on the company of involvement in the testing of the loco from 2010 onwards, its boiler having been re-built by Riley & Son Ltd at the ELR's Baron Street locomotive works. .

David Flood, 68 years old at the time and a long-serving ELR volunteer in many different capacities, was there on that day in January 2016 at Bury Bolton Street. For him, like many others, the sight of the locomotive provided a highly evocative experience: '*The Flying Scotsman* is a national symbol...it belongs to the people...I was

21 at the time when it looked like steam was set to disappear off the face of the earth. For me, it was a very sorrowful time which puts me back into nostalgic mode...It meant everything to me to be part of a crowd cheering the return of *Flying Scotsman*, taking pictures of it wreathed in clouds of steam.'

Peter Duncan steps down as Chairman at the end of 2015

At the end of his 15-year-long long spell as Chairman, Peter Duncan had achieved a huge amount. For example:

- managing the process of completion of the line from Bury to Heywood culminating in its opening to passenger traffic in September 2003
- securing lottery funding to enable the restoration and re-opening of Bury Transport Museum in 2010
- leading the company through a period of growth across many different fronts, rendering it successful as a profit-making organisation and at the same time able to plough financial gains back into the core railway business of the ELR and pay off various loans
- implementing various initiatives suggested by consultants to see visitor numbers grow from 100,000 to 200,000 per annum over a ten-year period

In succession, Mike Kelly was appointed to the post from 1 January 2016 onwards. Meanwhile, Peter Duncan continued serving ELR in the capacity of Signalling Director.

Notes

1. *Rossendale Free Press*, 11 September 2003
2. *Rossendale Free Press,* 13 February 2004
3. Nigel Jepson, *The Railway Town of Ramsbottom*, pp. 119-20
4. Spring 2007 *ELR News Magazine*, p.74
5. Summer 2008 *ELR News Magazine*, p.43
6. Autumn 2009 *ELR News Magazine*, pp. 64-5
7. Summer 2009 *ELR News Magazine*, p. 65
8. Spring/Summer 2011 *ELR News Magazine*, p.46
9. May/June 2012 *ELR News Magazine,* pp. 49-51

10.*Manchester Evening News*, 12 September 2014
11.May/June 2013 *ELR News Magazine*, p.63
12.January 2015 *ELR News Magazine*, pp. 89-91

Chapter 11 – Lockdown bites

Mike Kelly takes up post

Mike Kelly had first become involved with the ELR in his role as deputy Chief Executive of Bury Council. Subsequently becoming Chief Executive, his links with the ELR had grown even stronger. After retiring in 2015, Mike felt restless and offered his services, skills and contacts to help benefit the railway.

Invited to attend ELLR Board meetings, he commented: 'What struck me was that they were all people with a railway background, mainly in railway engineering. My background was completely different, but I certainly believed that I had skills that I could use to help the railway.' [1]

When after a relatively short settling-in period, he had been appointed as successor to Peter Duncan, Mike stated: 'I felt the role of chairman needed to focus on strategic and resilience issues; to be high profile; to be an identifiable figurehead for people to relate to, the voice of the railway with more engagement with volunteers, staff, visitors, politicians and other key partners.' [2]

One example of being higher profile was through introducing a '*Chairman's Blog – News from the Boardroom*' which he has continued to circulate on a monthly basis over the last eight years up to the present day with all back copies being accessible on the '*East Lancashire Railway: Home Page*'.

New ELR station opened at Burrs Halt

In May 2016, Mike Kelly was 'pleased to announce the finalisation of a deal to build a new, unmanned station in the heart of the Burrs Country Park, entering into partnership with a local Bury company, *Cheetham Hill Construction*...with a view to being ready to construct a five-carriage platform commencing in early June which is scheduled to take around eight weeks. We will also be constructing a shelter in the old style of the Lancashire and Yorkshire Railway.' As 'a local Bury lad', the owner and MD of the construction company CHC, Howard Chamberlain, expressed pride in signing up to the project.

On Thursday 13 October 2016, 'Burrs Halt' was officially opened on the East Lancashire Railway. The *Flying Scotsman* steamed into the new station at the head of the first passenger train to call there on the 08.45 service from Bury. A plaque was unveiled by the Mayor of Bury, Councillor Mike Connolly and the ELR Chairman, Mike Kelly, to commemorate the event.

On behalf of the ELR, Mike Kelly commented: 'I want to thank Bury Council, the Caravan Club and the Friends of Burr Society, all of whom have made very helpful financial contributions. The construction of the station will make it possible for visitors to Burr to arrive by train for the first time and allow holidaymakers staying at the Caravan Park to access the railway right on its doorstep.' [3]

In historical terms, the Burrs site went back as far as 1792 when Sir Robert Peel (father of the politician and later Prime Minister of the same name), had built a spinning mill there. Its wheels were powered by the River Irwell with a weir and canal constructed to carry water to them. As technology had advanced, the mill converted to steam power. Workers' cottages, dating back to those times, are still open to view, in similar-looking appearance as then. Mostly women and young children were employed at the mill, preparing and spinning cotton yarn.

The *Lancashire Cotton Famine* of the 1860s marked the end of cotton manufacture at Burrs. By 1880, the site was being used for paper making. In 1920, the complex had been taken over by the Star Bleaching Company. By 1925, Woodhill Road was constructed along the side of the canal feeder and a manager's house built, which is now the *Garsdale Public House*. During the Second World War, the site was used as a billet and later as an internment camp for Italian prisoners of war.

Demolition of the oldest parts of Burrs Mill had started in 1952, and in 1982 the rest of the mill followed, leaving only the workers' cottages and the chimney. However, Burrs had a new lease of life in 1986 when it was taken over by Bury Metro, being transformed into how it presently looks to visitors with the original workers' cottages refurbished to house amenities such as the *Lamppost Café*.

From the time of January 2017 onwards, the creation of the new 'Burrs Halt' enabled people travelling on the railway to access the surrounding Burrs Country Park with Stephen Holt acting as 'Passenger Liaison' officer. Covering 36 hectares of different wildlife habitats - including woodland, open space, wetland, ponds and waterways - Burrs has been awarded a coveted *Green Flag*. The *Irwell Sculpture Trail* runs through the park with four sculptures on display. Walkers, anglers, canoeists, birdwatchers and picnickers can enjoy the open environment. Burrs Park has unquestionably enhanced the range of options available to those travelling on the ELR network.

East Lancashire Railway – Volunteers' Charter

One of Mike Kelly's key priorities on election to office, from 1 January 2016 onwards, was to instigate a *Volunteers' Charter*. After wide consultation, a formal statement had been drawn up in December 2016 aimed at better defining the respective roles of those working on a voluntary basis for the ELPRS as opposed to paid employees.

The Charter 'set out the principles on which volunteering is organised and how effective relationships between the ELLR Company, paid staff and volunteers are built.' The ELLR Company's responsibility was defined as 'ensuring that all staff, including volunteers, are fit for the work they are being asked to do and for their health and safety at work.' [4]

New General Manager

On 2 May 2017, it was announced that Tracey Parkinson had been newly appointed to the post of ELR General Manager. Introducing herself to *ELR News Magazine* readers, she said: 'My love affair with heritage railways has covered over 25 years. It all started with a work placement at the *National Railway Museum* and a footplate ride at the North Yorkshire Moors Railway...My first visit to the ELR was when the *Duchess of Hamilton* was in her final steaming days...I have joined the ELR from the Talyllyn Railway, having thoroughly enjoyed my time working there and adding a bit of Yorkshire humour to the place.

'I have spent a fair amount of life at the North Yorkshire Moors Railway (NYMR) both as volunteer fireman and many years ago as their Marketing Officer. My proudest day there was to be on the V2 last steaming day, when tears were shed as *Green Arrow* is my favourite locomotive.

'My first impressions of the ELR have been what a lovely friendly place to be. We have plenty of challenges ahead including sustainable growth, quality of the passenger experience and raising sufficient funds to develop the railway and to provide training to enhance the skills for all our people.' [5]

'*Race the Train*'

One Sunday morning, the author arrived at 11 a.m. at Bury Bolton Street station to embark on a journey to Rawtenstall. I should add that several hundred others had also turned up as well as me. None of us would be travelling in the comfort of a railway carriage.

'*Race the Train*' (organised annually in recent times by ELR) is a running event covering an 11-mile (17.6k) course, devised to follow as closely as possible the route that an ELR train would conventionally take between Bury and Rawtenstall. As far as the idea of 'racing the train' is concerned, the engine runners are competing against on the day is scheduled to travel from Bury to Heywood before doubling back to Rawtenstall on a journey taking 1 hour 40 minutes. This sets the bar for runners – i.e. to aim to complete the run inside that time.

The nature of the event put me in mind of '*Choppy*' Warburton, noted Haslingden runner of the 19th century (whose exploits were described in an earlier chapter). How much this legendary athlete, who sprinted alongside the rail-track looking to take on steam-engines for pace, would no doubt have relished the prospect of participating in an event like this.

Re-living my own experience in 2017, the first section of the run seemed gentle enough until the route angled off down a footpath running adjacent to the rail-track. Given the amount of rain that had fallen midweek, the ground underfoot became rather treacherous. The First Aiders were having a busy time of it!

At Ramsbottom, a detour was taken round *Nuttall Park* before running up Nuttall Hall Road and turning left down Bury New Road. With my house looming into view, it was very tempting to drop off but I just about managed to keep going.

The route then headed on towards Edenfield, dragging up a long hill past Ewood Bridge, giving ample chance to recall the fact that the ELR is renowned for steep gradients. By the time I reached the top, ambition to '*beat/race the train*' had well and truly hit the buffers. Mercifully, Rawtenstall station finally came into view. Apparently, the 'competing' train had arrived twenty minutes ago and was now halfway back to Bury!

Putting the news to one side, I felt happy enough just to be able to flop down on a platform bench. Added relief came from Anna arriving on site to drive us back home and for me to sink into a hot bath tub.

30th Anniversary Event of 2017

On Tuesday 25 July, Ian Riley re-enacted driving locomotive '*Gothenburg*' along the same stretch of track from Bury to Ramsbottom that he had famously driven the train along, 30 years earlier to the day, in 1987. Sir William McAlpine (one-time owner of '*Flying Scotsman*' and currently serving as chairman of the *Railway Heritage Trust*) unveiled a plaque on Ramsbottom station recording this 30th anniversary which, as David Layland said during the course of a commemorative speech, 'meant so much to all the rail pioneers who had taken the ELR on the journey to where it is today'. A reception for the pioneers and invited guests was held at Bury Transport Museum. David Wright, Chairman of the ELRPS, in his welcoming speech, took pride in recounting the many successes to date of the ELR as a heritage railway company.

On Saturday, 22 July, the ELR had run a staff special to celebrate this 30th anniversary. On that occasion too, '*Gothenburg*' had done the honours. Diesel hydraulic locomotive *D832 'Onslaught'*, one of the first diesels to have arrived at the ELR, had also played a significant part in proceedings.

Fundraising project to secure *34092 'City of Wells'* for the ELR

Autumn 2017 witnessed the start of a fundraising appeal to purchase *ex-Bulleid Pacific steam loco, 34092 'City of Wells'* (built at Brighton in 1949), to make a permanent home for it at ELR. Back in 1964, *34092* had been withdrawn at Salisbury depot and deposited at Barry scrapyard where it was left rotting until 1971. That year, the rusting hulk had been purchased by a team of steam enthusiasts, Richard Greenwood, Graham Bentley and Guy Henderson (later, Guy's role in the partnership was to be taken on by John Adams) and moved to Keighley.

Following eight years of toil restoring *34092*, the locomotive was ready to return to operational use along the Keighley and Worth Valley Railway (KWVR) and many sections of the UK rail network until being withdrawn again in 1989. A further restoration programme was put in place which involved restoring *34092* to its 'as-built' appearance. '*City of Wells'* had returned to traffic once again in 2014, arriving as a visiting guest at the ELR in 2015. *34092* was always seen as a strong asset, hauling regular passenger services, starring at special events and also on *Dining with Distinction* trains, very much looking the part and especially so when sporting her '*Golden Arrow'* regalia.

In 2017, agreement was reached between the long-term owners and the ELR for the railway to buy the locomotive by the end of 2018 provided that the necessary cash could be raised. A massive fundraising campaign was launched to try to secure the purchase. After a great deal of effort from members, particularly project co-ordinator John Stephens, together with the generous donations of many hundreds of heritage well-wishers, the campaign's objective was achieved in March 2019 enabling the '*City of Wells'* to become a highly-valued new member of the ELR team roster.

Measure of progress made by ELR in 2017

By 2017, ELR had become the second most popular tourist attraction in Greater Manchester, attracting almost 190,000 visitors. In addition, it was the third most visited heritage railway in the country. Not that the company was at all inclined to rest on its laurels with plans for example moving forward in the Castleton direction.

An '"economic impact assessment" established that the ELR was now supporting 219 full-time equivalent jobs, up from 112 in 2008. ELR was stated to have generated more than £8.3m for the local economy in 2017, with fifty people in paid employment working on the railway, supplemented by an additional force of 780 volunteers.

Natalie Keaskin, sponsor from Network Rail, commented at this time: 'A forthcoming report will look at potential options to bring the heritage railway into Castleton and provide an interchange for passengers and services. This will allow the council to start discussions with stakeholders and potential third party funders.' [6]

The ELR decides to become a legally constituted entity

ELRPS Chairman David Wright put the rationale to members at the start of 2018: 'For some five decades the Society has been a club and achieved much in that time. But in an increasingly litigious world, I believe that it is time the Society should consider becoming a legally constituted entity. Indeed the debate has already started. Thus in 2018 the Council will consider how best to achieve this. This process may well be the most significant subject we have discussed for some time.' [7]

Following a ballot of members to determine if the Society should move from its current un-incorporated status to a Company Limited by Guarantee, the vote went overwhelmingly in favour of the motion with:

Total ballot papers returned: 1,855

Votes in favour of changing the Society status: 1,767

Increase in involvement of younger people engaged in working with ELR

During the course of a visit to the ELR carrying out research for a new book, railway author Andrew Martin wrote that 'the East Lancs makes a big effort to reach out beyond "Generation Steam". It has a "Learning and Audience" Development Manager, Matthew Britten, who has inaugurated an industry placement scheme for 16-18 year-olds. All of these students have since become regular volunteers on the line.'

In addition, Martin noted that 'the ELR has a primary education programme that brings 3,000 children a year to the railway. It has partnerships with seven local secondary schools, and a secondary education programme teaching '*STEM*' subjects (science, technology, engineering and mathematics) is in the offing.' [8]

Buckley Wells Development Progress Report: Autumn 2019

Taking a characteristically realistic view of matters, ELR Chairman Mike Kelly stated in 2019 that the Buckley Wells site, dating back to the mid-1840s, was 'not fit for purpose, and if we are to provide for the improved performance of locomotives, multiple units, carriages and wagons and staff welfare facilities into the future, we have to build modern facilities. The ELR is very fortunate to have such a large site, but it comes with a great number of problems to have to contend with, principally the need to repair and upgrade the structure, particularly in the light of a proposal for a Castleton extension.

Costed upgrades for the intended development of the site were broken into three distinct phases:

Phase 1: New carriage and wagon workshops at £4m.

Phase 2: Restoration of the Grade II - listed Workshops at Baron Street within the Buckley Wells Depot at £3m.

Phase 3: New running sheds and boiler workshops at £3m.

It was noted that the project as a whole, costing around £10m, would be a huge challenge for any organisation. It is a particularly big one for a heritage railway'.

§

Pandemic strikes

When Covid-19 struck, it affected all businesses with sledgehammer effect. In an article written in the Spring/Summer *ELR Review* 2020, then-ELRPS Chairman Chris Moore wrote: 'To say we are living in challenging and testing times would be an understatement. In March this year, the railway entered a period of lockdown. Currently, we have no indication when it will re-open. Events we were all looking forward to have been cancelled or postponed. Not only is this disappointing to those who had planned to visit us, it also has an incredibly significant impact on the finances of the operating company due to the loss of revenue and the need to refund advance sales.

ELRPS took steps in the meantime to mitigate the threat posed: 'The railway has launched an appeal fund, which the board fully supports...I have been amazed and humbled by the messages of support and encouragement received and the outpouring of love for our railway. As a member-driven society, we have always been prudent as to how we spend your monies and that judiciousness has allowed us to make a £125k '*Crisis Grant*' to the railway to help in this most difficult period in its history.' 10

Meanwhile ELRPS President Pete Waterman played a pro-active role in urging train fans and supporters to donate to the ELR Support Fund to allow the railway and its 800 volunteers to re-open after Covid-19 had had the effect of forcing the company to close its doors.

It was later announced that the ELR had 'received vital and timely financial support of £194,300 from the *National Lottery Heritage Fund* to help it recover from the impact of Coronavirus...The new funding will be used to undertake essential track maintenance, cover the additional costs incurred with making the railway Covid-safe and upgrade its online presence.' 11

'Good to be back'

Fierce and relentless as the Covid lockdown had been, recovering patterns of activity eventually opened up again the following year. In his Report for the year, David Wright stated: '2021 has been challenging for us all. After weekends of crew competence assessments in April and May, trains began running again...And it was so good to be back.

'It was a very busy time though making sure that staff who had worked with the company pre-Covid were brought back up to speed, let alone ear-marking time and resources for the purpose of training new recruits. The process was still more complex for the reason that, as another effect of Covid, people's approach to carrying out voluntary work had unquestionably changed in the meantime. But the pandemic has left a fundamental legacy. Many people from all walks of life have sat down and posed the question: what do I really want to do with my life? Some have changed how and where they work. Some have changed what they want to achieve.' [12]

For his part, Mike Kelly stated: 'Nationally, Covid has massively impacted on people's way of life and has, possibly forever, changed the way we risk assess our future engagement interactions with other people. Heritage railways generally have experienced reduced numbers of volunteers, with some not returning, shielding or simply new volunteers holding back. Whilst the ELR is showing some reduction in the number of working volunteers, it's clear the railway is seeing only the regular volunteers turning out to help in the running of services and events with more and more paid staff being drafted in to fill the gaps.' [13]

Margaret and Dave Wilson

Visiting Summerseat station on a Sunday morning following the end of lockdown, I managed to catch up with Margaret and Dave, two veteran ELR volunteers who had originally started tending the station gardens there from 1993 onwards. Both said it felt great to be back. Where they live is a 20-mile journey away. Travel restrictions had of course been in force during the pandemic. It had worried them how the grounds might have deteriorated during the intervening months but luckily not too much had suffered. Watching today as the two of them went about their work in customary hi-vis jackets, Margaret and Dave appeared very much 'back in the zone'.

As well as their continued involvement at Summerseat, the husband-and-wife team's commitment to the ELR still stretched as broadly as ever. Dave still also served as an ELRPS Board Member. Apart from acting as Volunteer Liaison Officer, Margaret continued to look after ELR's central record system. Like Dave, she too served as an ELRPS Board Member.

ELR Long Service Awards

By way of honouring the outstanding contributions made by so many volunteers over the years, a special presentation evening was held at Bury Transport Museum on 20 October 2021. At the event, 58 staff and volunteers were awarded plaques for long-term service to the ELR. Most notably, the four longest-serving volunteers, Lois Vevers-Hatton and Peter Lord (007 membership number!) for 52 years and Richard Law and Phil Bailey for 51 years, all received gold awards for dedicated services. Significantly, this group of four spanned the whole period from when the original ELRPS had been founded in the 1960s right up to the present day. This was certainly a fitting way to pay tribute to the "survival of the fittest"!

The 58 awards handed out on the night represented 2,000 years of service. Although the central purpose of the event was to honour the massive achievement of all those receiving the awards on account of retrospective service, the opportunity was not lost to stress the need for new volunteers to come forward to swell existing ELR numbers down the line.

Buckley Wells Project update – February 2022

Receiving planning approval from Bury for an updated £12m-costed ELR Development Plan at Buckley Wells, Mike Kelly commented: 'Our latest vision is for Buckley Wells to be an engineering centre of excellence, building on our apprenticeship programme...It is the critical and indispensable base for storage and maintenance of historic locomotives such as *Flying Scotsman*.' [14]

'Return to normal'

ELR Vice President Keith Whitmore reported that from summer onwards it had been a "return to normal" with such as *Thomas Trains* running again...'Well attended Diesel, Steam and *DMU* galas have also been able to return and the icing on the cake must be the privilege to be able to not only run *Flying Scotsman* along the line, but for visitors to be able to board the footplate...I nearly lost my voice on the second day of *Scotsman* at Heywood with the sheer number of times I outlined to our visitors the history associated with the loco.' [15]

Santa Special events were back in full swing with ELR Chairman Mike Kelly commenting: '*Santa Specials* have been running for 35 years. Last year's *Specials*, the largest such event put on in the country by a heritage line, saw 42,000 people of all ages attending. Our aim each year is to make the event bigger and better in terms of bringing the Christmas magic and experience to the railway.' [16]

Filming projects continued to take place which provided a welcome income stream, including a *Black Horse* advert for *Lloyds Bank*, *Ridley Road* and *Sherwood* for the *BBC* and *Red Rose* shown on *Netflix*. The Lloyd's Bank advert proved to be a particularly interesting venture. The scene, featuring the Black Horse and *Flying Scotsman* was filmed at Irwell Vale on the ELR.

'Richard Law and Sean Lea, two of our ELR Directors, visited the Lloyds Bank (separately) in Bury to see if the bank would reproduce the photo for use at Bolton Street and Irwell Vale stations to mark the occasion. Bank manager Andrew Mills took up the matter and the request went all the way up the company's management chain before Lloyds came good and provided the railway with framed photos.' [17]

Other more recent events and awards achieved

In a later *ELR Review*, Mike Kelly gave updates on other events that were freshly emerging in post-Covid times: '*Halloween* is now supplemented with activities in the Bury Transport Museum. *Day Out with Thomas* was re-designed in 2021...whilst *Peppa Pig* was a new sell-out event concept with licensed characters and entertainment focused at the museum...the prospect of attending a celebration of the 100th anniversary of LNWR/LYR brought visitors to the ELR in droves.' [18]

Always a marvellous event and great money-spinner, *Santa Specials* were shortlisted in the *Marketing Lancashire Awards*. In seeking to find out more about '*Santas*,' the author found himself blessed one day to be granted opportunity to speak with 'Father Christmas' himself no less! The fact that 'enactor' Peter Beetham wasn't togged up in his £800 outfit made the experience a little less daunting all-round. Peter said being something of a natural extrovert helped in order to play the role. Still, unexpected situations could arise: 'While children enjoy being given a present, parents get perks such as a miniature bottle of *Bailey's*. On one occasion, I was surprised when a child confided in me that he was grateful for his present but that his mother would like to have some more "babies". The whole carriage was in stitches...I took it upon myself to re-fill her glass with another shot of *Bailey's* and it did the trick!'

Awards kept coming the ELR's way. *Trackside* won the *CAMRA* award for best pub in Bury. *Dining with Distinction* was the *Trip Advisor Travellers Choice* for 2022. *DMU 50455* won the 2022 *Railcar Association Award. 'Pug' 19* was shortlisted in *Steam Railway Magazine* for rapid restoration and involvement in L&YR centenary celebrations. The ELR also scooped a national award for its re-design of the company's website.

Notes

1. Andy Coward, 2018, *East Lancashire Railway*, pub. Mortons Media Group Ltd p.50
2. As for above: p.50
3. May 2016 *ELR* News Magazine, p.58
4. January 2017 ELR News Magazine, pp.75-9
5. September 2017 *ELR News Magazine*, p. 21
6. *Rochdale News*, 13 July 2018
7. January 2018 *ELR News Magazine*, p.9
8. Andrew Martin, 2022, *Steam Trains Today,* pub. Profile Books p. 353
9. Autumn 2019 *ELR News Magazine*, p.9
10. Spring/Summer 2020 *ELR Review* p.6
11. Autumn 2020 *ELR Review* pp. 8-9
12. Winter 2022 *ELR Review* p.6
13. As for Item above – p. 81
14. *Bury Times*, 23 February 2022

15. Winter 2022 *ELR Review* p. 15
16. *Bury Times*, 1 December 2022
17. *Chairman's Blog* – November 2021
18. Winter/Spring *2023 ELRPS Magazine* p.16

Chapter 12 - Fit for survival for the future?

The '*City Valley Link*' proposal

At the same time as welcoming a 'return to normal', Keith Whitmore also alerted ELRPS members to a new threat facing the Company, that of 'Rossendale Council putting forward their ill-thought out proposals for a commuter train across the valley.' [1]

In October 2022, the '*City Valley Link*', a scheme drawn up on behalf of Rossendale Council, with support from Lancashire County Council, argued the case for a comprehensive railway system to 'once again connect Rossendale and Lancashire'. The business case had been submitted to the Department of Transport for its consideration.

The *CVL* scheme projected an end-to-end journey time of 44 minutes from Rawtenstall to Manchester, as opposed to the current peak time bus/car journey-time of up to 90 minutes. A service of two trains per hour at peak times and one per hour in the off-peak was seen as a further incentive. The cost, including station improvements, was estimated at £80m, with an annual operating cost in the region of £3-5m. A connection to Metrolink was envisaged via a pedestrian interchange at Bury.

Outlined in two phases, the first would utilise the existing heritage line between Rawtenstall and Bury. Phase 2 would use that between Bury (Market Street) via Heywood and thence on to Manchester Victoria. It was argued that the new form of rail link would contribute to the growth of the local economy by creating around 5,000 new jobs over the next 25 years with improvements in connectivity bringing the visitor economy within easy reach of the 2.8m people living in Greater Manchester. In addition, environmental benefits would accrue with the new rail link having the potential to remove around half a million car journeys made annually, causing a dramatic reduction of fuel emissions into the air.

The *CVL* submission to the Department of Transport inevitably posed a threat to the ELR in terms of its seeking to transform the existing heritage line into a largely commuter-orientated 'modus operandi'. Keith Whitmore's response to the *CVL* proposal put things more graphically: 'At times it seems as if we are being used as a political football to prove a point to the Department of Transport... and at the same time being forced to defend our very existence rather than working with Rossendale to make Rawtenstall a worthy tourist destination. How many more times do we have to make the case that without the ELR we would never have seen the regeneration of Ramsbottom that was really suffering from empty shop units and dereliction to the thriving tourist town it is today. We will, I am afraid have to keep up the pressure to ensure that these mad-capped ideas which threaten our very existence remain a line on a map never to see the light of day.' [2]

'Rover ticket' experience

Bearing in mind points made above by Keith Whitmore, the author took it upon himself to carry out a spot check on some of the issues raised, signing up to a 'rover ticket' - which allows opportunity for a train passenger to stop off anywhere en route during the course of a day's travelling on the ELR.

Interestingly, railway writer Andrew Martin had carried out a similar journey in recent times, describing findings in Chapter 7 of his book *Steam Trains Today,* his initial impressions being as follows: 'Bury Bolton Street is a bruised-looking station of red brick and BR Midland Region maroon. It's half 1950s and half Victorian...There's a compelling anti-glamour about the East Lancs, which has more diesel engines than any other preserved railway. This was a steam day, but I hadn't come to Bury for the engines. I'd come to make a point about the future of preserved railways...' [3]

Martin further added 'The East Lancs is firmly rooted in its locality..."That's the thing about our line", the train guard told me as he checked my ticket: "Bury, Ramsbottom, Rawtenstall, they're all *towns*, and the railway has done a lot to help them." It might, in fact, have done too much, which has given people ideas.' [4]

What I see on a rail journey

My day's journey starts at Bury Bolton Street boarding *80097* (a *Class 4*, originally built in Brighton in 1954) to travel to Heywood, where I am grateful to station master Bob Howorth for pointing out many things, including the level-crossing gate about 200 metres distant which marks the end-point of the ELR line. Beyond this, the regulatory body is Network Rail. Consultations are still on-going with Castleton Township as to line extension. Platform options remain to be agreed, entailing possibility of a parallel ELR platform either to the west or south of Manchester Road Bridge.

Glancing in the opposite direction, towards Heywood itself, the spacious car park commands attention without though any real sight from here to be had of the town itself. I am reminded that the siting of the station, like others at the time, was largely determined by the nearby location of industry in the mid-19th century, very little of which has survived, leaving the Heywood station of the present day rather isolated-looking.

My concentration returns to what is happening in front of me on the platform, watching with interest how *80097* is being unfastened from the front carriage. A young man, face buried under a *Peaky Blinders* cap, jumps down from the engine footplate and disappears under the train to carry out the uncoupling procedure, thankfully emerging back to platform-level unscathed. Next moment, I notice the engine is chugging along the other side of a short stretch of double track, down past the stationary carriages. This is aimed at enabling it to resume lead position for the return journey to Bury.

Those now looking to board the train consist mainly of grandparents and very young grandchildren. Two generations removed, both seem equally spellbound though by the sight and hissing sound of steam released from the majestic, black *80097*. Within a quarter of an hour of having arrived, departure time looms. Hopping on to the train, my intended next stop is Rawtenstall, terminal point at the other end of the 12-mile line. Arriving there, it inevitably brings back memories for me of the '*Race the Train*' event that I'd run. It's been a far more comfortable journey getting here to-day!

There are good hospitality features at the station such as the '*Buffer Stops*' bar. On the platform itself, a refurbished carriage, the *Rawtenstall Café* serves meals, cakes and sweets. My intention though is to take a wander round town and check out the general experience for those travelling ELR. With this in mind, I abandon *80093* to its return journey, intending to catch a later-scheduled train to travel back down the line.

As at Heywood, the message hits home here in Rawtenstall that the siting of railway stations in the mid-19th century was gauged to meet freight-carrying needs. Walking along New Hall Hey Road, I come across the old *Hardman Mill*, serving nowadays as the *Hardman Business Centre.* Exploring the present-day site, I struggle though to pick out any visible reference-points to the past, for example by way of information boards.

Aiming towards the town-centre, the confluence of major roads (at the foot of the A56) makes passage difficult. Having an idea to visit *Whitaker Museum*, I realise though that I would need to take the underpass to reach the bottom of the A682 Haslingden road and then trek a mile or so uphill before reaching it. I abandon the idea, deciding to travel there by car another day.

On this later occasion, the *Whitaker Museum* and grounds is well worth the visit. The original house, known as *Oak Hill*, had been built in the early 1840's by one of the wool-manufacturing Hardman family, George, amidst 28 acres of parkland. The present-day museum provides a most interesting range of exhibitions illustrating Rawtenstall's past history. The mansion remained in the hands of the Hardman family until 1900 when it was bought by Richard Whitaker. He too was a mill-owner who had donated the property, including the grounds, in 1902 for the benefit of all those living in Rawtenstall.

However, recalling my visit to Rawtenstall on the 'rover ticket' day, I had found my journey on foot from the station a tortuous undertaking, not least lacking helpful 'sign-posting'. Although it is obvious Rawtenstall has sites worth visiting, including the converted *Lambert's Mill* and the *Rossendale Ski Centre* for the more adventurous, the route from the station to the town-centre could have been made a lot more helpful and attractive. Some of Keith Whitmore's words echoed in the mind!

As things stand, more definitely needs doing to promote a stronger connecting thread between station and town. This is despite the fact that Rossendale Council had in December 2020 adopted a 2020-2030 '*Visitor Economy Strategy*' aimed at creating stronger links between the ELR and Rawtenstall Town Centre through the promotion of walking routes and other marketing/PR activity.

Taking all sources of information into account, it would appear that Rossendale Council in present times leans more heavily towards developing its *CVL* project as opposed to strengthening its commitment to ELR as a heritage line.

Ramsbottom

Much has been written to this point about the advantages that accrued to this town from the opening of the ELR's heritage line between Bury and Ramsbottom back in 1987. On the occasion of the author visiting Ramsbottom today, it cannot be denied that the station has a friendly, welcoming feel to it, fostered not least by the warm way in which Station Master Chandra Law 'meets and greets' passengers on the platform.

As far as access from station to town is concerned, it is an obvious blessing that the town-centre is just a stone's throw away. Within a minute or two, the ELR traveller can have reached the foot of the main thoroughfare, Bridge Street, and a range of inviting shops and cafes. The short time it takes to access the town is obviously a strong factor in the undoubted appeal of visiting Ramsbottom town from the station. What is also evident though is the amount of supportive background information available, in the form of information boards and plaques, many of them put up by the very active Ramsbottom Heritage Society, aimed at helping the visitor learn more about the culture and history of the town.

Continuing support for the ELR's on-going projects

Over recent times, the ELR has continued to receive encouragement for its current on-going projects from Bury and Rochdale Councils as well as the Greater Manchester Combined Authority. For example, Councillor Eamonn O'Brien, leader of Bury Council, after commenting on the size and the scale of the operation at Buckley Wells, said: 'The ELR has a long history of operating in Bury, and we have seen its development since the railway was rescued from dereliction back in 1972. Some 50 years later, we are pleased and proud that the ELR sits at the heart of our community here in Bury.'

Likewise, Councillor Neil Emmott, leader of Rochdale Council, after visiting the site, stated: 'The history of the ELR and its value to our local community is there for all to see...This major North West attraction is an important asset and we wholeheartedly want to work with the ELR going forward to ensure it has a sustainable future as a successful guardian of 'living history' for future generations.' [5]

Visit to Buckley Wells

Strongly aware of the part Buckley Wells Works has played in the history of the ELR going back to the mid-19th century, I took it into my head to visit the South Bury site one day, not at all sure what to expect.

On a cold winter's day, towards the end of 2022, I arrived there with frost encrusted on the ground. First impression was of a desolate site. It just looked like everywhere was closed down. Trudging round the vast area only heightened a sense of futility as to why I had ventured here on little more than a whim of curiosity.

Thinking to head back to where Id parked my car, my luck took a turn. Chancing across a tucked-away cabin-area, I tried the door and was surprised to find it unlocked. Entering uncertainly, I picked up sight of a man sitting at a desk. Lifting his eye off the computer screen, he took casual note of me. Feeling I owed an explanation for my presence, I blurted out something to the effect that I was writing a book on railways in East Lancashire.

Unsure what the reaction might be, I was thankful to hear a welcoming response, the man introducing himself as Andy Hardman:

"deputy head of Traction and Rolling Stock". Conversation ensued and before long, seizing hold of a bunch of keys, he was kindly offering to take me on a tour of the site.

During the next half-hour, Andy showed me round buildings going back to the 1840s and also the range of engines and carriages currently on site, all at various stages of having work put in on them. The scale of the challenge to maintain rolling stock under present conditions looked considerable. It was plain to see why there were plans to upgrade facilities.

Back in his office, Andy showed me old ordnance survey maps going back to the 1840s. Then, most courteously, he accompanied me back to where my car was parked. Along the way, he pointed out a particular building that we hadn't come across on the tour we'd just been on. In casual-sounding fashion, he dropped in that it was where '*Flying Scotsman*' was housed.

'I could let you in if you're interested?

'*Flying Scotsman*' did you say? ' I don't need second invitation.

From the outside, the 'shed' in question hardly looked spectacular. Nor did it on the inside. There only appeared to be rusty-looking carriages hanging around, looking as if they were queueing up for a lick of paint. Moving further inside, I heard Andy let out in a dry style of delivery that we were approaching the *Flying Scotsman*.

Holding my breath, it seemed utterly remarkable to venture like this into the exalted presence of the world-famous *Scotsman*... a 'Pegler' moment if ever...beholding the bright green engine!

I listen spellbound as Andy passes comment on *Flying Scotsman*. Tellingly, he doesn't refer to elements of its record-breaking history but instead dwells on the practical engineering side, stating that what we are looking at today is a whole world away in mechanical terms to the original engine built in 1923.

It is now a hundred years since then and, tellingly, Andy explains that virtually every part of the original engine has been replaced along the way to keep the *Scotsman* operable. Over time, prodigious amounts of money have been spent on it by a series of owners. Illustrating the point further, with the *Scotsman* static before us, Andy homes in on the one or two few remaining original engine parts, those that bear

Scotsman's distinctive original engine number – *4472* – which was of course later to become *60103*.

Thankful to be given this forensic analysis, it does not diminish one jot the frisson felt from coming across this giant of a majestic steam engine lying as if asleep at the back of this shed.

At the end of the visit, I'm left with plenty to reflect back on. I have been amazingly lucky today to catch a wondrous glimpse of the *Scotsman* in hibernation. Although resting up for the moment, it wasn't to be for long with the great *Scotsman* scheduled to roar back into action on ELR lines in March 2023.

Visit to Castlecroft Museum

Feeling still very much on a high, I make a similar impromptu visit to Bury Transport Museum a few days after. Castlecroft is of course where it all started after the ELRPS moved here from Helmshore in the late 1960s.

I have visited the site before but not in recent times. Today my attention is focused from the start on the imposing sight of *LNER A4 'The Union of South Africa'* - enjoying pride of place at the front of the museum. Originally numbered *4488*, the engine *60009* had been built at Doncaster Works in 1937. On 24 October 1964, it hauled the last booked steam train from London King's Cross before being withdrawn from BR service on 1 June 1966.

Rescued by John Cameron in July 1966, '*Union*' was preserved for a while on his *Lochty Private Railway* in Fife, Scotland before being placed back on the national network from 1973 onwards. It was from May 2022 onwards that '*Union*' had been placed on static display here at Bury Transport Museum. Still owned by James Cameron, I learn that it may be called back to Scotland sometime soon. Given the likelihood of this happening, the Museum is keen though to replace *'Union'* with some similar live footplate experience for the benefit of visitors.

The next exhibit to be encountered is the tribute to Sir Nigel Gresley. Born in 1876, he rose to become one of Britain's foremost steam locomotive engineers and the designer of many famous *LNER*

Class A1 and *LNER Class A4 4-6-2 Pacific* engines, including *Flying Scotsman* and *Mallard.*

After several early jobs with the L&YR, Gresley had been made Works Manager at the Newton Heath depot in 1903. In 1905, he moved to the Great Northern Railway (GNR) as Carriage and Wagon Superintendent. In 1923, he was appointed Chief Mechanical Engineer of the newly-formed LNER and knighted in 1936 for his services to railways. Sir Nigel Gresley died in 1941. Recently, in 2016, commemorating seventy-five years since his death, a statue was put up in honour of Sir Nigel, standing in the concourse of King's Cross Station, London.

These two main exhibition pieces – paying respect to the '*Union of South Africa*' and Sir Nigel Gresley – both serve to illustrate the strong continuing interest the ELR has with regard to honouring the history of rail transport.

'*Trackside*' meeting with Tracey Parkinson and Lee Kenny

On the same day Andy Hardman showed me around Buckley Wells, General Manager Tracey Parkinson had happened to arrive on the premises. I'd have liked to have a chat but she had other business to attend to at the time. She did invite me though to meet up with herself and Lee Kenny (Head of Traction and Rolling Stock) later on in the week at the *Trackside*..

Tracey was unavoidably delayed on the day but Lee was there. I asked him how he had first become involved in railways. He said his interest had developed at the age of 12 after his uncle had taken him trainspotting at Manchester Victoria. Living then in Ramsbottom, he was amazed at the impact the opening of the Bury-Ramsbottom line had had on the life of the town. He had been with the ELR 26 years and been in the traction and rolling stock department throughout, having become Head of the Department some ten years ago. At the moment, he was also serving as Deputy General Manager

When Tracey arrived, a three-way conversation began, tending to centre around issues Tracey said were facing the company at the moment. For example, the soaring cost of fossil fuels put a question mark over the continued viability of steam and diesel engines alike. The ELR was about to publish detailed statistical evidence, highlighting the scale of such concerns. Mike Kelly was in process of writing a paper on the matter.

End-of-2022 'assessment'

In his seventh annual report, Mike Kelly presented to Society members his assessment of where the ELR stood in the post-Covid context with two central questions posed:

- What had been the impact of Covid in business terms?
- Where did the situation leave the Company for the foreseeable future?

As may have been expected, figures produced showed a sharp dip for the most severely Covid-affected year of 2020 with regard to 'visiting numbers', 'turnover' and 'profit/loss'. However, given ELR's continued rebuilding following lockdown, 'visiting numbers' (even if not back to the heights of 2019) had risen back significantly in 2022 with an additional 40,000 guests visiting.

Provisional breakdown figures for 2022 indicated that event days were again crucial in generating sustainable levels of revenue for the railway. For example, the *Santa* season had amassed revenue of £1.1m excluding ancillary income. After the refurbishment of *Trackside*, the pubs were expected to generate income of £770k. 'Efforts have been made to run some non-train events. These include *Peppa Pig*, an evening with John Cameron and '*Union of South Africa*', and Halloween *Carn-Evil*, with some *Wizards* events on Sundays.' [6]

Effects of added fuel costs

'General costs, excluding utilities and fuels', the report continued, 'have increased by an average of 9% in the year. A new utility contract was negotiated by Paul Bonello, but the best price tendered resulted in costs tripling from £100k to £300k per annum. The even more threatening price-rise came with coal which has shot up from £249 per ton at the start of the year to a high now of £420 per ton. Gas oil has followed a similar pattern. Like all heritage railways, running costs have increased significantly...Whereas in January 2022, the average running cost per day was £1,824, by December of the same year, the figure had risen to £4,929 per day'. [7]

In the ELR's '*Strategy Summary: 2020-2030*', it was noted that 'the Government ban on domestic coal by 2023 and power stations by 2025, will force heritage railways to import coal which will double associated costs.' [8]

In due course I was lucky enough to have chance to talk with Mike Kelly in person. He showed me various other items focussing on the fuel issue. One was a letter sent to all heritage companies in 2022 by Steve Oates, Chief Executive of the *Heritage Railway Association*. Despite the gloomy overall picture, there appeared possible ways forward. For example, processes relating to alternative use of *BioCoals* continued being trialled. It was noted though that 'trials conducted at the Keighley Worth Valley Railway (KWVR) indicated that more work needs to be undertaken to achieve a suitable 'coal' for larger and longer railways. In addition, the results of chemical analysis are awaited to understand the effects of the 'coals' on copper and steel fireboxes and other parts of the boiler.' [9]

Buckley Wells Development Update

On a more optimistic note, ELR members were informed that 'almost 90% of the planning conditions for the site are ready for submission... In partnership with Transport for Greater Manchester and Bury Council we have been liaising with them to construct a new access road north to south on the eastern side of the site...A new volunteer group has been set up to manage the 7-acre wildlife area to improve the biodiversity of the area in partnership with *Bury Grammar School*'.

Furthermore, 'a successful application has been made to the *UK Shared Prosperity Fund* thanks to the support of Bury Council. We have been awarded £50,000 to help us finalise the work on completing the planning condition in readiness for the start of preparing the site for construction works.' [10]

Optimistic hopes for the future

At the start of 2023, Mike Kelly stated to members: 'In July the ELR will celebrate 36 continuous years of operation and I am sure the challenges back in 1987 were no less daunting. As each year dawns, we remain optimistic and confident that with good planning and management, and the continued support of our fantastic staff and volunteers, we have got a lot to be excited about. With the valued support of Society members and its Board, 2023 will be another successful year for the ELR!' [11]

With the last train of the Christmas/New Year season having taken to the rails on 2 January 2023, the traditional lull in terms of public programme operated thereafter, providing chance to prepare for the advent of the new 2023 calendar starting in March.

Although Rossendale and Lancashire Councils had said they were hoping for a response from the Department of Transport to their *City Valley Link* proposals by early Spring 2023, the ELR remained intent on getting on with 'business as usual' in the meantime. For example, what more exciting spectacle could there have been to set the New Year programme rolling than the return of '*Flying Scotsman*' in its centenary year?

Flying Scotswomen!

A special slot was built in to the *Scotsman's* 2023 centenary tour schedule taking place on ELR lines between March 1 and 25: 'In another major first in its proud history, *Flying Scotsman* was on 8 March crewed by an all-female team for three round trips to mark *International Women's Day*'.

'The ground-breaking crew comprised three of the railway's volunteers in Linda Henderson, Charlotte Instance and Steph Elwood along with Beth Furness from Network Rail who drove the *A3*'. Chandra Law, in her capacity as station master, also played an important part in facilitating the passage of '*Scotsman*' on the day.

As mentioned previously, Linda Henderson had first begun volunteering work back in 1993. 'Throughout the years, she had taken on many different roles at the railway including dispatcher, signal operations manager and in 2017; she became its first-ever female main line locomotive driver.

'Steph joined the ELR in October 2021 with a background in maintenance and repair...she was soon placed on a fast-track course and passed her firing exam in September 2022, becoming the second-ever female fireman on the heritage line.'

Meanwhile, 'Charlotte had come to the railway in 2021, following in her great-grandfather's footsteps when she joined the steam crew as a cleaner...since when she had worked her way up to the coveted position of locomotive driver.

National Railway Museum director Judith McNicol added: '*Flying Scotsman's* centenary is a chance to celebrate the history of this famous locomotive, but also to reflect on how far we've come in terms of women's opportunities in rail and what still needs to be done.' [12]

Volunteer Dismissal Controversy

The '*Flying Scotswomen*' story had portrayed women's representation in a very positive light but unfortunately the ELR became the subject of adverse national press coverage for dismissing female volunteer Joanne Crompton following her complaint about 'misogynistic behaviour and discriminatory treatment'. Ironically, she had recently been short-listed for the 2023 *Railway Award* for *Inspirational Woman of the Year.* At the time, 'the company denied unfair treatment'.[13]

Two separate issues seemed to develop. One was the feeling expressed in an 'open letter' sent to 'staff and volunteers' by Mike Kelly that Joanne Crompton had somehow over-stepped the mark by putting views on social media, and by so doing had caused the company reputational harm. For this, she appeared to have had her volunteer status revoked.

On the substantive issue that was raised by the complainant, a procedure was eventually put into effect whereby an independent officer investigated the matter with the complaint of 'sexual harassment' being upheld. It was also agreed that a policy should be drawn up making it explicit to all employees that such behaviour was unacceptable. The services of an experienced HR officer should be sought to assist in the setting up of training programmes. The effectiveness of this action can only be judged over time.

ELR visit from Michael Portillo

Michael Portillo paid a special visit to the ELR as part of Series 14 of his '*Great British Railway Journey*' TV programme, taking a trip on the line in the company of Richard Law. Reflecting on the loss of local train lines in the 1960s and 1970s, he imparted the following historical perspective: 'Britain had won the war but...focused on modernising the home country, building a network of motorways... The railways couldn't take the competition from the roads. Heritage lines like this one remind us of what we lost following the *Beeching Cuts*.'

Standing at the cross-roads

The cost of fossil fuels, by way of powering steam and diesel locomotives, has continued to carry serious implications as far as affecting bottom-line profit margins of ELR operations across the board is concerned. At the same time, it is appreciated that ecological considerations seriously need to be taken into account.

In his '*Chairman's Blog*' of July 2023, Mike Kelly announced that 'Tracey Parkinson is leaving the railway after 6 years in charge... expressing a wish to move on and explore new opportunities. Mike paid the following testimony to the contribution she had made: 'Throughout her time with the ELR she has been an exceptional and transformational General Manager in what has been a very challenging few years both during and after the pandemic'. Meanwhile, Mike also announced that 'Lee Kenny is stepping up to the role of ELR's Acting General Manager, with a future review of the position to take place in the new year'. By way of update, Lee was to be appointed General Manager on a permanent basis in January 2024. [14]

While, at the present time of writing, nothing further has been heard regarding the future of the *City Valley Link* proposals, new transport plans were announced in October 2023 by Bury Council to seek to effect further major local railway developments. With £68m in hand to roll out plans, one proposal is to introduce new technology so that Metrolink services can be used on the previous rail network between Bury and Rochdale via Heywood. The scheme, which would see the former Calder Valley Line restored, was earmarked for government funding through the '*Restoring Your Railway Fund*' but this was pulled in January due to rising costs.

According to Bury Council, *Transport for Greater Manchester* (TGM) is currently developing plans that, apart from meeting clientele need, break new technological grounds. This involves developing plans that would see a rail link between Heywood, Rochdale and Oldham using tram-train technology. All of this would have great benefit for the ELR, in terms of enabling the company to realise its long-term aim of becoming connected up to the mainline rail network.

Bury Council further said: 'We are exploring the potential for a connection between Heywood and Bury, with the longer-term aim of linking to the existing Metrolink networks in the north of Manchester and improving connectivity to the Calder Valley line. 'The focus of the project will be to create the next generation Metrolink vehicle, tram-train infrastructure. The proposal will provide new technology that will allow Metrolink vehicles to operate on existing heavy rail lines as well as the Metrolink lines.

'Councillor Eamonn O'Brien, leader of Bury Council said 'This new strategy comes at an exciting time for transport: Greater Manchester, with bus services coming under local control for the first time in almost 40 years. If we are to realise our vision and our regeneration plans, we need a state-of-the-art transport system that is affordable, safe, reliable and well-maintained. We need our transport network to unlock new gates for development, to promote health and well-being through active travel and to help meet our commitment to having fossil-fuel free travel by 2038.' [15]

2024 events to date

'The much anticipated visit of LNER A4 60007 *Sir Nigel Gresley* and pioneer British Railways Standard class locomotive 70000 *Britannia* (along with LMS Jubilee 45690 *Leander* which had been regularly used during the winter) drew big crowds on and off the trains over the weekend of 15-17 March 2024.'

Following on from this, 'on 28 March, LMS 3F *Jinty* 47298 featured on a 3P20 Photo Charter paired with a box van and a pair of *Mark 1* carriages. The charter took advantage of lineside clearance at a number of locations, including just north of Irwell Vale station and Burrs.

'Always a major ELR event, this year was no different with performances of all kinds up and down the line...The set hauled by *City of Wells* included a flat wagon, with a pair of gun carriages to convey the impression of a troop train. Throughout the weekend, the *Bluebird Belles* trio sang their hearts out at Bury Bolton Street.' [16]

Rounding my research off on an ELR Volunteer Recruitment Tour

On Saturday 11 May, I availed myself of the opportunity to attend a Recruitment Tour. The ELR schedules a number of such events in its calendar to encourage members to step up to working for the company in a volunteer capacity. Arriving in the entrance-hall at Bury Bolton Street Station at 10 am on the day, I and the rest of the party of ten were welcomed by Tour leader Glen Newport at the start of an itinerary that would last six hours until 4pm. This long because there were so many places to visit!

The whole idea was to take you 'behind the scenes' and provide opportunity to talk to staff and volunteers who already work on the railway. Although details can vary on any particular day on operational grounds, our party got to visit the admin office, *Bury Transport Museum*, *Carriage and Wagon works* and the *Signalling Department* where Director Peter Duncan (one-time ELR Chairman 2000-15) gave an excellent presentation in characteristic droll manner.

Then it was the *Loco Works* and sidings at Baron Street before catching a train and taking on board accounts given by people 'on the move'. Our last port of call was at Ramsbottom station where, received convivially by station master Chandra Law, we also had chance to visit the Signal Box.

It amounted to an absorbing day all-round. Tour leader Glen Newport and the team around him did the ELR credit through being polite and informative about everything they showed us - a great advertisement for what there is on offer for would-be volunteers!

Eventually, when the clock ticked round to 4, I found myself having to admit to Glen that the main reason I had come on the tour was to include mention of the experience in the book I was writing. As for committing to volunteer work, I promised to keep the option open. When it came to providing more formal feedback, I stated I had enjoyed the visit tremendously and been greatly impressed by what I had been given the chance to see 'behind the scenes'.

§

This book's story started in the 1800s describing how the achievements of pioneers such as George Stephenson had stimulated the *Railway Mania* of the 1840s and an intensification of rivalry between a rapidly-proliferating number of companies to gain the competitive edge. The harsh law of the "survival of the fittest" had led to the demise of the original East Lancashire Railway in 1859.

Despite East Lancashire lines swapping hands between different railway companies throughout following decades, nothing was ever to prove as dramatic as the scale of cutbacks that came about from the *Beeching Cuts* of the 1960s. Following the widespread closure of stations and rail lines that took place in the early 1970's, the ELRPS, to its enormous credit, proved itself a model of persistence in ploughing a lone furrow for the best part of 20 years before success was ultimately achieved in 1987 with the opening of the heritage line in 1987 between Bury and Rawtenstall. ,

Although the original ELR was fated to come to an end in 1859, at the present time it is held that the modern-day ELR heritage line has every good reason to feel confident regarding future prospects.

Notes

1. Winter *2022 ELR Review* pp. 15-17
2. As for Item above – p. 17
3. Andrew Martin, 2022, *Steam Trains Today*, pub. Profile Books, pp. 351-2
4. As for Item above – p. 354
5. As reported in '*Chairman's Blog*' – September 2022

6. Winter/Spring *2023 ELR Review*, p.11
7. As for Item above, p.12 8
8. *ELR Strategy Summary*: *2020-2030*, p.6
9. Steve Oates, *'Coal Supplies-Update Position'* – a letter to members of the Heritage Railway Association, p.1, dated 04.03.22, kindly provided by Mike Kelly.
10. Winter/Spring *2023 ELR Review* p. 16
11. Spring 2023 ELR Review, p. 48
12. Brian Sharpe with Robin Jones, 2023, *The Flying Scotswomen*, an article in *Flying Scotsman Centenary Special*, pub. Mortons Media Group Ltd., pp. 143-5
13. The Telegraph, 4 May 2023
14. As reported in *'Chairman's Blog'* – July 2023
15. *Transport for Greater Manchester* – October 2023
16. Summer *2024 ELR Review* pp. 58/9

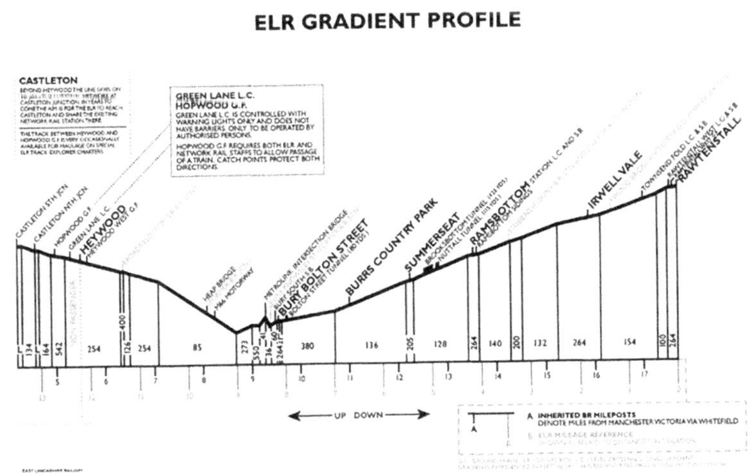

ELR Gradient Profile

Sources

Surprising Lancashire (Chris Aspin) published by *Helmshore Local History Society* 1988

Lancashire 1750 to 1850: The First Industrial Society (Chris Aspin) published by Carnegie Publishing 1995

Railways in East Lancashire (Martin Bairstow) published by Martin Bairstow 1988

The East Lancashire Railway (Martin Bairstow) published by Martin Bairstow 1993

The East Lancashire Railway Official Guidebook (Richard Barnett) published by East Lancashire Light Railway Co. Ltd 2015

The Holcombe Brook Branch (Michael Blakemore) published by Michael Blakemore 1975

The Lancashire & Yorkshire Railway (Michael Blakemore) published by Ian Allan Ltd. 1984

The Four Great Railways (Michael Bonavia) published by David and Charles 1980

Opening of the East Lancashire (Bradshaw's Railway Gazette) 1846

Bygone Heywood (John Cole & Grahame Fish) published by Rochdale MBC 1982

The Holcombe Brook Branch (CA Cowan) A Branch Line Society Publication 1965

The Decline of Railways in Bury and Rossendale (Andrew Coward) published by Andrew Coward 2013

The Revival of Railways in Bury and Rossendale: Back in Time: 1987-1999 (Andrew Coward) published by Andrew Coward 2016

East Lancashire Railway (Andy Coward) published by Mortons Media Group Ltd 2018

Scenic Railways – 10: Heritage Railways (Ed. Pip Dunn) published by Kelsey Publishing Ltd 2023

History of the English Railway 1820-45 - Volume II (John Francis) published 1851

A History of a Station – Heywood (John Gwilliam) 1970

The Railway Comes to Bury – Communication Developments in South-East Lancashire (Harry Hanson) 1969 BA dissertation, University of Manchester

Harrison & Sale's Guide to the East Lancashire Railway: 1849

A Personal History of the East Lancashire Railway Preservation Society up to 2010 (Harry Hatcher) Unpublished – copy received courtesy of Peter Duncan (ELR Light Railway Company Chairman 2000-2015)

Heywood (Hannah Haynes) published by Chalford 1997

The Reshaping of British Railways (HMSO) 1963

A Regional History of the Railways of Great Britain Volume 10 – The North West (Geoffrey Holt) published by David and Charles 1978

Railways (Julian Holland) published by Rydon Publishing 2007

Come On You Rams (Nigel Jepson) published by YouCaxton 2020

Ramsbottom's Revolutionary Doctor (Nigel Jepson) published by YouCaxton Biography 2021

175 Not Out (Nigel Jepson) published by YouCaxton 2022

The Railway Town of Ramsbottom (Nigel Jepson) published by YouCaxton 2023

Lancashire Railways (Mark Jones) published by Countryside Books

Journal: Volume 1 (Fanny Kemble) 1835

The 'Flying Scotsman' published by the London & North Eastern Railway 1925

Memories of Nuttall Village (K. McCarthy) 1992

The Lancashire and Yorkshire Railway - Volume I (John Marshall) published by David and Charles, series 1969-72

Steam Trains Today: Journeys Along Britain's Heritage Railways (Andrew Martin) published by Profile Books 2022

The Lancashire & Yorkshire Railway in the 20th Century (Eric Mason) published by Ian Allan Ltd. 1954

The Nostalgia Collection 54 – East Lancashire Railway Recollections (David Mather) published by Silver Link 2015

British Railways in the 1950s and '60s (Greg Morse) published by Shire Library 2012

The Lancashire & Yorkshire Railway – A Concise History (O.S. Nock) published by Ian Allan Ltd. 1969

Lancashire: Steam's Last Stronghold (David Packer) Sutton Publishing 2005

Nuttall – Ramsbottom's Lost Village (*Ramsbottom Heritage Society*) 2020

Ramsbottom Reminiscences (*Ramsbottom Heritage Society-* edited by Andrew Todd) 2022

The East Lancashire Railway (RW Rush) published by The Oakwood Press 1983

The East Lancs Walk (Tom Schofield) produced privately by Tom Schofield

Flying Scotsman – Centenary Special (Brian Sharpe with Robin Jones) published by Mortons Media Group Ltd 2023

A History of Edenfield & District (John Simpson) published by *Edenfield Local History Society* 2003

Zeppelins Over Lancashire (Peter JC Smith) published by Neil Richardson 1991

Lost Railways of Lancashire (Gordon Suggitt) published by Countryside Books 2003

Railways in and around Bury (Jeffrey Wells) published by Challenger 1995

East Lancashire Lines: Bury to Heywood and Rawtenstall (J Wells & EF Bentley) published by Foxline 2000

The Bacup Branch (Ramsbottom-Stubbins-Rawtenstall) as part of the series '*Branchlines of the L & YR*': No. 3 published by the L & YR Society 1985

The Holcombe Brook Branch as part of the series '*Branchlines of the L & YR No. 6* published by the L & YR Society 1988.

§

ELR magazine articles – courtesy of ELRPS volunteer Kevin Owen, working in the *Emporium* at Bury Bolton Street station, I was able to gain access to an almost full set of magazines going back to the 1970s

Mike Kelly's '*Chairman's Blog*' – 2016 to present day

Newspaper articles from a range of sources including: *The Telegraph, The Mirror, Manchester Chronicle, Manchester Guardian, Manchester Evening News, Bury Times, Bacup Times, Liverpool Courier, Rochdale News, Ramsbottom Observer, Rossendale Free Press, Burnley Evening Star, Blackburn Standard, Manchester Chronicle, Bolton Chronicle*

Various other magazine entries including: *Lancashire Life, Railway Times, Ramsbottom Heritage Society*

Turnpike Trust Statements & Accounts

Manchester, Bury & Rossendale Company minutes

Ramsbottom Heritage Society magazine articles

Ramsbottom Heritage Society minutes of meetings – courtesy of RHS Secretary John Leyland

Copies of '*Ramsbottom War News*' (Life in Ramsbottom during WW2)

City Valley Rail proposal – '*A Better Connected Local Economy: The Case for the City Valley Rail Link*' – Rossendale Council: Autumn 2022

About the Author

ORIGINALLY FROM SHEFFIELD, Nigel Jepson has lived in East Lancashire for the last 30 years. His interest in local history has led to four publications in recent times:

- *The History of Ramsbottom United Football Club (2020)*
- *Ramsbottom's Revolutionary Doctor – Life & Times of Peter Murray McDouall (2021)*
- *The History of Ramsbottom Cricket Club (2022)*
- *The Railway Town of Ramsbottom (2023)*

He also currently works with publishing firm "*Alan Godfrey*" on its '*Historical Ordnance Survey Map*' project series – having contributed accompanying texts for four different editions in 2024: *Ramsbottom; Stubbins; Tottington; Irwell Vale/Lumb.*

Nigel's background career is in education – as a secondary school head teacher for 30 years across schools in Chesterfield, Todmorden, Haslingden, Bradford and Bolton, as well as subsequent, interim posts abroad in Dubai (2016) and New Delhi (2018).

Presently, he is researching into the history of schools locally with a view to publishing a book (working title - '*Slates, Zeppelins and SATS'*) exploring the history of education in Ramsbottom, Holcombe and Stubbins from mid-19th century to present day.

As a member of the *Lancashire Local History Federation*, Nigel delivers talks to local history societies for example in recent times at Ashton-under-Lyne, Edenfield and Ramsbottom. On behalf of 'Heritage Days', he has led local 'walks', most recently in September 2024 around Chatterton relating to the events that unfolded during the "weavers' uprising" (aka "Chatterton Riot") of April 1826.

Nigel has also written novels, for example:

- *The Inspector and the Superhead (2000)*

- *Cut and Run (2006)*
- *In a League of His Own (2011)*
- *Speed is of the Essence (2015)*

In leisure time, he enjoys 'keep-fit', having run marathons in Manchester, Liverpool, Belfast, London, New York, Venice and Dubai up to 2019. Since Covid though, distances have adjusted to 5 and 10ks!

* 9 7 8 1 9 1 5 9 7 2 6 4 4 *

BV - #0117 - 041124 - C32 - 216/140/13 - PB - 9781915972644 - Gloss Lamination